FORENSIC
LEADERSHIP

FORENSIC
LEADERSHIP

Changing the Culture of a Nation

TRENT T. NORTH

AuthorHouse™
1663 Liberty Drive
Bloomington, IN 47403
www.authorhouse.com
Phone: 1-800-839-8640

Published by AuthorHouse   04/27/2012

ISBN: 978-1-4685-7436-4 (sc)
ISBN: 978-1-4685-7437-1 (hc)
ISBN: 978-1-4685-7438-8 (e)

Library of Congress Control Number: 2012905940

CONTENTS

FOREWORD

The Forensic Leader contains numerous thoughts I wish to pass on
to my daughters. Some of the memories they will have of me will be
of my talking on a cell phone or leaving home to attend meetings. It
has been difficult for my girls to understand what other things their
daddy does outside of his regular job. Hopefully, Alecia and Alexis will
gain insight into my life experiences and thereby, become better leaders
themselves.

I believe every person leads in some area, at some point in his or
her life. It is my hope that the understandings I have gained along the
way will enable them to avoid some of the hidden hazards of leadership
and realize success.

I grew up in government housing in Carrollton, Georgia. Those early
years in "the projects" were enriched with experiences that undergirded
budding leadership skills. Since then I have been privileged to serve
in a variety of leadership positions within my community, including
governmental, private, and community boards. Each duty held its own
challenges and rewards.

At the age of twenty-four I was elected to our County Board of
Commissioners where I have served the citizens of District One and all
of Carroll County, Georgia for twenty years. Throughout my five terms,
I have served as vice chairman for both a predominantly Democratic
board and a predominantly Republican board.

For five years, I served on the board of directors for Citizen's Bank
and Trust. I also served in an advisory capacity to the Bank of North
Georgia during one of the worst times in history for the banking

industry. In addition I was named Chairman of the West Carrollton Enterprise Zone.

Besides the ongoing work as County Commissioner, I currently act as chair and founding member of the Carrollton Men's Home. I am Chairman of the Board for Mt. Zion Missionary Baptist Church, Inc. I sit on the board of directors for the Carroll County Chamber of Commerce. I also have a seat on the Real Estate Foundation Board for the University of West Georgia and the university's Board of Trustees. Finally, I serve on the Tanner Medical Foundation for our local hospital.

All these assorted leadership experiences has yielded a thorough development of skills. My growth as a leader certainly disciplined personal relationships, finances, and health. Although readers may lead in fewer areas, the knowledge I have gained enables me to assist them in their various leadership quests.

ACKNOWLEDGMENTS

Without the support of family, friends and co-workers, I could not have completed this book. My family and friends supported me in immeasurable ways, and for them I am deeply grateful.

A heartfelt thanks to my wife Toya who knew that the book would be one more added responsibility for me, yet she and our two daughters have been very supportive throughout this process. I am also very appreciative of my good friend, Dr. Vickie Cox—Edmonson. As an author, Dr. Cox—Edmonson shared the process she used when writing her book and suggested a number of printing companies. Her assistance was invaluable.

Before I began writing <u>Forensic Leadership</u>, I shared my vision of the book with my good friends Jackie Lowe and Chris Bonner. The vision for the book began in the winter of 2005. They both motivated me along the way and are glad to see the book complete. They both have held the vision with me, and I am very appreciative.

When I began writing the book, I knew I would need an editor, and I wanted someone who understood me. Thanks to my wife Toya, who steered me in the right direction by suggesting a former colleague and employee of mine, Debbie Williams. Having worked with Debbie for over 20 years, I was confident I had an editor who not only understood me but spent six years with me at the middle school as my assistant principal, so she was familiar with my work. Debbie did an excellent job of editing my work. Debbie's editing of the first draft was invaluable and she deserves a lot of credit.

For a second editing, I turned to my former college professor, Dr. Martha Ann Saunders, who was chair of the English department when I attended the University of West Georgia. I only had one wish, but I did not share it with her—I did not want her to use a red pen. Even though not discussed, she instead used a pencil and provided great feedback for the book. Her wisdom was very insightful and appreciated.

When I was ready for feedback on the content of the book, I turned to my mentor and former colleague, Jackie Fillingim. Jackie deserves credit for expanding my vision of what this book could and should be. We not only had good conversations about the content, word choices, and the number of chapters, but the order of the chapters as well. Finding the time to write more chapters was challenging; however, the book is much better as a result. I am very appreciative of her patience, her time away from family and her wisdom.

I would like to also thank Marva Bell, a teacher at the middle school, who previewed and provided good editorial feedback on the book and book design. Her passion for writing and her insight as an educator and a business owner was valuable.

Much thanks goes to my leadership team members at the middle school for their inspiration: Debbie Williams, Laura Malmquist, Nicolas Miller, Kenya Elder, Shannon Miller and Beth Cater. When I was working on my introduction, Kenya Elder provided wisdom. Throughout the book I tried to capture the spirit of many of our conversations.

Several people have supported this project and provided words of motivation and wisdom along the way and I want to say thanks. Thanks to Adova Hobson, Dr. Charlie Rouse, Dr. Michel Flood, Dr. Howard Seeman, Dr. Kent Edwards, Donna Derbecker, Shawanta Jones, Mercy Hernandez, Susan Mabry, Dr. Samuel Mercer, Sharon Stanford, Julianne Foster and Dr. Mary Hooper.

A special thanks to my baby sister, Tabitha North, for taking the picture that is shown on the cover.

I am very appreciative for the former staff of the middle school where I served as principal. The four-hour going away celebration they provided for me motivated me to complete the book. It inspired me because they conveyed to me that they "got it". Each direct and subliminal message I was attempting to teach, they got. I do not think the book would be as strong without the six years spent at the middle school. Also, I am grateful for Ms. Malmquist's efforts to get every staff member to write in a journal for me. I could not include every journal entry in the book; however, prior to and at the end of each chapter I included a letter from some of the journals. I want to thank the teachers for allowing me to share their insights. I changed the names to protect the staff members and chose cities I had visited that reminded me of the individuals for their locations.

A special thanks to Jennifer Finnell who has worked with me on this project since 2005. She has been patient with me as I have changed directions at least four different times. Thanks Jennifer!

A very special thank you to my daughters, Alecia and Alexis, for being patient with their daddy. Thanks for not pouting as much when I could not watch a movie with you because I needed to work on the book. I am very proud of both girls, and I know they will grow up to be great leaders. I wrote this book with the two of them in mind, and I hope that they will both read this book with pride.

I owe much to Toya North, my wife, for all her support on this project and every other project. She has been an avid supporter of mine for over 20 years, and I am most appreciative. I thank her for allowing me to consume our kitchen table for six months straight. I also thank her for pushing me and continuing to believe in me. She is a very special person, and I am glad to have her in my life. I would not be who I am without her influence.

Chapter 1

CHANGING A CULTURE

Mr. North,

I am not sure where to start. I began my career under your guidance, and I cannot imagine how I am going to make it without you as my principal. I can recall you speaking with my mother and ensuring her that I would be safe and you would take care of me if she allowed me to work for you. Now, we both have the upmost respect for you.

You have taught and encouraged me more than you will ever know. I can honestly say that you've greatly influenced my career, and the success that I've experienced as a teacher. I attribute much of my success to you and your leadership. It is not every day that one has the opportunity or takes the time to say thank you, so I want to say, Thank You Mr. North. Thank you for hiring me as a first year teacher and giving me the opportunity to build relationships and shape minds, hearts and lives. Thank you for helping me establish myself within this community that I can now call home. Thank you for believing in me when I didn't believe in myself, and for motivating me to purchase a home. I am proud of my investment.

Please continue to inspire and lead those who will follow. Great educators impact the lives of many, just as you have had a positive impact on my life.

Atlanta, Georgia

In 2005 I had the honor of being appointed the principal of a new upper elementary school. When I received the phone confirmation, I was very excited and confident in my abilities to continue the tradition of success for which the school system was known for. At the time of my appointment, I was at the peak of my career and believed that I was well-respected in my community. Since I had leadership experience, I felt confident about my abilities to lead successfully. I thought, "I am primed for school leadership!"

The system that gave me the opportunity to lead represents a very unique and progressive school system. The system is very rich in technology and is well respected throughout the state and nation. It has received significant recognition for its excellence in the three A's: Arts, Academics and Athletics. Five schools had comprised the district: an alternative school, a high school for grades 9-12, a junior high school for grades 6-8, an elementary school housing grades K-5, and a Pre-K Center. The system was completing a new middle school building to house grades 4 and 5, thus reducing the size of the current elementary school. The floor plan for the edifice was designed to eventually house grade levels 4, 5, and 6. Expected enrollment for the new school was approximately 500.

The new middle school sits on a hill and overlooks the entire school system campus. It would be the newest building in the system. When the telephone call came from the superintendent conveying that he and the school board were in agreement that I serve as the principal of the new middle school, my wife and I rejoiced with excitement. We knew that this was a rare and remarkable opportunity to demonstrate my skills and, more importantly, to serve teachers, students, parents, and the community. However, this period of pure excitement was short lived.

Prior to the first students coming into the building, I began to fully realize some of the challenges that I would face as a principal. The first challenge which was unexpected, and fully unappreciated, was the fact that I would be seen by many as the first African-American principal to lead a regular education program in our system. Even though my appointment was a historical accomplishment, I did not want race to be the focal point of my administration. This was a topic that I had previously learned could be an instant job killer if openly discussed in any community.

The support and respect I believed that I had earned in the community was tested very early. I was a proud product of the local government housing projects and a well-respected leader in the African-American community. However, due to the existence of a psychological phenomenon known as *internalization oppression*, many in my own community saw my appointment as principal as positive, but remained unsure whether I had the necessary skills to be successful. Their lack of confidence in my ability to give advice, to lead, and to provide instructional guidance to African Americans would be impeded by my culture's belief that white is right and black is wrong. Although I knew this prior to the appointment, but because I was never in a position where the final decision was solely mine, I could always dismiss their doubt as an individual's lack of confidence in me personally.

I remember when my pastor stood up in church and made the announcement about my appointment. He noted how very exciting it was that once again one "of our very own" had broken tradition and forged new territory in our community. He reiterated that I would be the first African-American principal over a regular education program in the school system. The gentleman sitting next to me jokingly responded, "Couldn't they hire someone black?" referring to my fair skin. Was he serious, or was he kidding? My appointment did not occur because the color of my skin is very light.

I received my board appointment in June and was very excited. I was attending an NAACP banquet in November. The event was an annual event to raise funds for the non-profit organization. I attended the banquet alone as my wife had decided to stay at home with our two daughters. As I entered the room with much excitement, I was approached by a school board member from a school system outside my district. However, the individual's melatonin was darker than mine. When she approached me about my promotion, the word "Congratulations" did not come out of her mouth. Quickly as if she had been waiting to say this, she said, "Wow! Kissing the Superintendent's butt finally landed you where you wanted to be! How does it feel to become a principal and to know that you earned it by kissing the superintendent's butt?" In disbelief and total shock, I laughed it off as I often do when I feel pressured or stressed so that I would not lose my cool. I proceeded to get in line to be served with two good friends, Adova Hobson and Anita Jones. I recall Adova looking at my expression and asking, "Who spoiled your night?" I shared with her what had just occurred and responded, "Regardless, I will not let her comment spoil the evening."

My struggle with African-Americans who questioned my abilities, my skills, and my content knowledge did not end there. Many assumed that because I was now the principal that I could undo all of the wrongs in our school system, the neighboring school systems, the community, and to some degree in America. If someone needed a job, then it was my responsibility to find them a job as a custodian in my building or in another building. There was a mistaken belief that my title allowed me to influence other principals to hire and employ teachers, custodians, and paraprofessionals. One lady applied for a job at another school in our system. To assist her, I called the principal and put in a good word for her. The principal interviewed the perspective teacher but eventually selected someone else. I received a subsequent telephone call at home and cannot begin to describe the superlatives she used to blame me. She and her family were very clear, and they believed that she did not get the job because I did not want her to get it. This was an upsetting event to my wife who answered the call and to me.

My new-found struggles with African Americans were not the only immediate concern. I quickly realized that some in the white community saw my appointment as a token position as well. Even though I considered them my friends and I still do, comments were made such as "There's nothing wrong with being hired because of your color, you deserve opportunity." or "Someone had to be the first. We're glad it's you." All of this conveyed that they too saw my appointment as serving to meet a quota.

I remember meeting with a parent before the first child sat in my building as the parent talked with me about the placement of her incoming 5th grader. The parent proceeded to request that her child be placed in a specific teacher's class and wanted to suggest the names of other students to be placed with her child. When I conveyed to the mother that the middle school does not honor requests nor do we allow parents to decide who will be in the class with their children, the mom stated what I believe many others were quietly saying and thinking, "We knew you would be different and not like the rest of the principals." It was refreshing to hear her utter these words. I assumed that some might have that mindset, yet in my deepest prayer, I never thought someone would have the courage to convey that to me. On one occasion, I was standing in the front lobby with my two assistant principals and a mother came in needing assistance. I was standing between my two assistant principals and it was very clear this was a problem that needed to be handled by the principal. The associate principal interrupted the parent and said, "This is Mr. North. He is our principal and he will have to help you." The mother proceeded to ignore the redirection of the associate principal and continue a monologue with her. Once again, the AP conveyed to the mother she could not assist her and referred her directly to me as I stood shoulder to shoulder with her.

The struggle with my faculty was also detected very early. I was fortunate enough to meet with my entire faculty during the summer prior to the opening of the school. Despite that, initially many of the teachers, paraprofessionals and support staff did not view me as the principal and instructional leader. My faculty was not a new faculty. After negotiations with the elementary school principal, I was excited to welcome many of the 4th and 5th grade teachers from the current elementary school. In addition to the teachers and paraprofessionals, I was able to select one assistant principal from the elementary school and hire a second administrator. I knew I had a great faculty and I looked forward to working with each one.

Even though the school board gave me the authority to serve as the principal, many did not perceive me as the principal prior to school starting, and for several months into the school year. However, no one can give you leadership through a title, it must be earned. Many saw either the associate principal who was a more familiar face to them or the new assistant principal as the principal and saw me as the assistant principal. I was convinced then and am still convinced six years later, that the actions of my staff were not intentional but reflected habits learned from society. On one occasion, I can recall instructing teachers to perform a necessary task, thinking that my request alone was sufficient. Upon receiving my request, on numerous occasions teachers would check with the AP's to see if the task really had to be completed, not realizing that my Associate principal would share their inquiries with me.

In addition to African-Americans and white Americans, it did not take long for me to realize that the Board of Education as a group was convinced that I had the competency and the skills to lead the middle school but that some at the district level saw me merely as a political asset. Some at the district level believed that my strengths were primarily my political and people skills. I did not recognize that at first. Leadership would say things like, "You know you don't have to get involved. You can let your curriculum person handle the curriculum and you can just stand back." I missed the innuendo of that comment. Although the principalship was my second appointment, I continued to miss the subtle messages about my capability.

My first appointment was as principal of the alternative school, and shortly after the announcement was made I almost turned it down. At that time I was working as an assistant principal at the elementary school. As I was sitting in front of my office, one of the fifth grade teachers approached me and said "Congratulations. I hear that you are hiring my husband's best friend from Auburn." She said, "Yes. He's going to be teaching science for you."

You must understand that in my system, the principal selects staff for hire, then recommends to the Human Resource via the board who to hire. Politically, we all know that there are times when there is someone that the leadership wants you to hire and you hire them. Even when that occurs, out of common courtesy, the leadership will notify the principal first so that there is still the perception that the principal is the one hiring. I was furious. I can recall going into my office and calling the district office and saying "Whoa. Wait a minute. You've got the wrong one. If you want someone in face only I can't be the principal, and I don't want it." The response was "No, that's not the way it is. This is a misunderstanding. I just interviewed him and liked him and wanted you to talk to him." Of course, I went ahead and hired him (I'm not a dummy!), but I missed that first subtle message. I had to come to the realization that leadership saw my assets as political ones.

When most principals or other leaders are hired to lead an organization, there is what we call the "honeymoon phase". That is a time when leaders have some freedom and flexibility to invest in getting the organization moving in the direction they want it to go. However, it appeared that in addition to my concerns with the African-Americans and the perceptions of the white community, I was not going to experience a honeymoon phase. That did not bother me, but when I realized that my enrollment numbers were going to be higher, and I would be provided with fewer services than the previous school's administration, I began to be concerned. In a scheduled meeting with the leadership, I pointed out that my enrollment was going to be 570 instead of the 505 originally projected. I knew daily exactly what my numbers were, as my secretary and I enrolled students and had that information constantly in front of us. Even at 505 students, I had fewer teachers working for me with larger numbers in classrooms than the prior school's administration.

At that time the leadership directed me to talk to the principal at the elementary school that had previously been responsible for that grade level. It was not clear why as a principal sharing enrollment numbers with leadership, one would insist that I consult with the principal at the previous school. Of course I did as directed, but I could not understand why someone would appoint me as principal if they did not have total confidence in my ability. The principal at the lower school felt awkward because although she confirmed my projections, she was fighting to get six new teachers at her school as well. I was requesting only two teachers, and that would still result in larger class sizes at my school. The principal declined to call the leadership even though she agreed with me, as she was struggling with her own numbers. I was then directed to go meet with the junior high school principal, regardless of the fact that I had been principal of the alternative school four years longer than the junior high school's principal had been at that position. This meeting echoed what the elementary school principal had said and still I was not assigned the requested teacher slots. However, the elementary school received two slots more than she had requested. Not only did the leadership send me to consult with other principals, but I was required to meet with the director of special education regarding the placement of my students. This was irrelevant to that fact that I had placed students at the elementary school for five years longer. Also, she had never been a principal and scheduled all students. It was not that leadership was deliberately depriving me of my responsibility, as many people would assume. It was clear that throughout my relationship with some at the district level, leadership saw me as a public official not as a school leader. Regardless of how well my school would perform or what I did, the middle school's success was always attributed to other factors: my school was small, or I had great teachers, or a combination of other elements contributed to the school's success, but none of it was attributed to my personal leadership skills. It seemed evident that there were fellow African-Americans, and white peers as well as leadership at the district level who did not actually possess confidence in my abilities. Despite evidence of respect and affection within both African-American and white communities, and gestures of acceptance by my leadership, subliminally there remained a genuine disbelief in what I truly brought to the table. I experienced all this as I prepared to open a new school.

Also, the achievement data for the fourth and fifth grade students I was about to inherit was dismal. If the middle school had been assessed independently during the spring before the new school opened, the 4-5 school would not have made adequate yearly progress (AYP). In addition to not meeting state benchmarks, the fourth and fifth grades were the two poorest performing grades in the system.

I was faced with an African-American community who loved and respected me yet didn't truly value what I brought to the table, continuing to view me as "Trent from the block". There were those from the white community who had an endearing respect for me because of my accomplishments in the community and because they are proud that I have progressed from the projects to middle-class America, yet some still viewed my appointment as a token position.

I was at a crossroads. Do I bow out or do I formulate a strategy to create the best school/organization in our system? Only my wife and two other individuals knew that I considered leaving for a less demanding job at the Georgia Department of Education after only three months into that first school year.

As you can imagine, my initial excitement was diminished. Nonetheless, my enthusiasm for students remained. I could not fail; there was too much at stake. The opportunity to model how to lead and change a culture compelled me. I Knew I had a lot of hard work ahead of me, and that failure was not an option. Changing the culture within the organization and community, developing leaders, establishing a successful program and formulating genuine relationships that extended beyond the workplace were my tasks. This was the beginning of forensic leadership at the middle school.

Mr. North

Where do I begin? I have been with you since you began in administration in 1996 at the elementary school. Now here we are working on 22 years of experience and some of my best times, in fact, a lot of my best times have been while working with you. I have so many professional growths that I have to thank you for. Beginning with a welcoming ethos, The Fred Factor—I do try to be "A Fred", Leadership 101, The Undisputable Laws of Teamwork, and none other than Who Moved My Cheese. Well, you are certainly moving my cheese.

I have many different emotions right now, but the most important one is that I am completely happy for you making this change. The maze we have traveled through has blessed us greatly. I am glad I got to move along with you to discover the true handwriting on the wall. Thank you for the professional growth as well as the personal growth. I will always be thankful for your time, attention, consideration, humor and friendship. I will miss your insight on a day to day basis, but I look forward to your work at the board office. My prayer is for you to enjoy the change, saver the adventure and taste of new cheese.

Bologna, Italy

Chapter 2

FORENSIC LEADER

Mr. North,

I call you Mr. North because I respect the position and role that you have as the leader of CMS. It may seem too formal, but I know my place. Really, when I think about who you are and what you represent, I call you a man of faith. Early in the mornings, you walk the halls pondering life's greatest question. Lord, how do we make it this day? Just as He is about to give you his divine answer, someone stops you in the hall and wants to bend your ear. Thankfully, you manage to convey to that individual that you value their concerns. That's just how you do things.

Harvey S. Firestone said, "The growth and development of people is the highest calling of leadership." I perceive that it has always been your goal to produce more leaders, not followers. I marvel at how you are able to blend left and right brain people together to produce an awesome staff of people. I call you leader.

I have had the pleasure of working with you for five years now. WOW! I count it all joy. All I really want to say is Thank You!! Thank you for enabling and empowering me to have courageous conversations. Thank you for your constructive counsel and guidance. When it's all said and done I can truly say, I call you friend.

As you begin a new chapter in your life, remember to lean not to your own understanding, but in all things acknowledge Him and he will direct your path.

Anguilla

From early history, philosophers have attempted to define the term leader and determine the qualities that distinguish an individual as a leader. I believe a leader is any individual who demonstrates the ability to organize a group of people to achieve a common goal. The ability to lead is not derived from a title nor does it need to originate from formal authority. Mobilizing a group of two or more individuals toward a common purpose requires leadership, and that capacity exists within each of us. The question becomes: when it is your time, will you choose to lead?

Forensics is most commonly defined as the application of a broad spectrum of sciences to answer questions of interest to a legal system. This may be in relation to a crime or a civil action. The word forensic comes from the Latin forēnsis, which means "before the forum." In Roman times, a criminal charge meant presenting the case before a group of public individuals in the forum. Both the person accused of the crime and the accuser would give speeches based on their sides of the story. The individual with the best argument and delivery would determine the outcome of the case. This origin is the source of the two modern usages of the word forensic—as a form of legal evidence and as a category of public presentation.

For our purposes, forensics will be defined as skills in investigating and establishing facts or evidence at the smallest or most simplistic level possible. It requires one to focus on the smaller fragments of an organization to get to the underlying causes or truths. Everyone can develop a forensic perspective. For some this ability comes naturally. For others who are more right-brain dominant, this skill may require that individuals train themselves to become less holistic and more detail oriented.

In the past, many leaders have been described as either visionary leaders or detailed leaders. Visionary leaders do an excellent job of motivating employees, customers and the media to support their ideas. A visionary leader is a people-person who may be charismatic, is very persuasive and may possess an innate ability to discover the best in everyone. It is important to note here that most people do not simply support good ideas; they also follow and support an individual. A visionary leader is rarely short on words or ideas, delivers a better impromptu speech than a prepared one, and is often referred to as a leader with charisma. However these same leaders may become frustrated when the time comes to bring their lofty ideas to reality. A visionary leader is viewed as laid-back and can be very knowledgeable about almost any topic. When appropriate, visionary leaders prefer to use personal examples or stories to convey their message. The example may be a personal one or refer to any individual who is part of the discussion. It is most common for a visionary leader to approach a problem from a holistic view. This leader is considered to be imaginative, flexible and spontaneous.

Detailed leaders are viewed as very hands-on and are most valued for their ability to attend to details. Tasks and situations are approached from an analytical perspective and practical precision drives many of their decisions. When dealing with employees, they are considered to be consistent and fair to all. If an employee has read the employee handbook, he knows the consequences prior to entering the office. These leaders may be viewed as very knowledgeable and masterful regarding specific topics. Detailed leaders refrain from personalizing conversation and will not permit anyone who is a part of the discussion to do so. Everyone is treated equally with very few exceptions for special circumstances. Detailed leaders are hardworking, cautious, well-organized and very practical in their approach.

An effective leader in the new millennium must master the visionary aspects of leadership as well as its detailed components. The balanced combination of these two concepts comprises 'Forensic Leadership'. Forensic leaders possess the skills to systemically impact and lead an organization by the ability to be both creative and analytical at the same time. They are logical and holistic in their approach to problems. Although a Forensic Leader may be masterful with people skills, the rules and expectations are all implemented equitably. This leader works to hone his skills the way Kobe Bryant practices to perfect his basketball skills.

The image of a satellite orbiting Earth provides an effective symbolic representation for a forensic leader. The satellite has the ability to view the entire world at one time and quickly process available data. It has the ability to capture images of meteors that pose a potential threat to Earth. While viewing Earth as a whole, the satellite can simultaneously capture images of individual continents at many different levels. In addition to having lenses to capture large scale images, the satellite also has the ability to narrow its focus to a single address. This narrowed image allows it to focus on a specific home or at a particular individual who is standing at the specified location at a certain time. This aeronautic device is both holistic and precise at the same time, and forensic leadership is demonstrated by the satellite instrument. Forensic leaders understand the organization's current status and have several creative, yet practical methods for moving it forward. They are able to relate to and interact with a board of directors and probe to learn of their individual and collective needs, while at the same time strengthening relationships with employees in the field and tending to their needs. I believe that it has been forensic leaders who have made our country a great nation and a world power.

As principal of the middle school, it was essential that I serve as a forensic leader. For example, when I attended a Chamber of Commerce Board of Directors' retreat, I needed to strategize with public and private business leaders for solutions for our local economy. That work could ultimately lead to better collaboration among existing businesses, as well as the potential recruitment of new industry to provide more jobs, and to create a platform to educate business leaders within our community about the current status of public education. As one of only three educators sitting at the table, I often wanted to inform the Chamber Board about changes or exciting movements occurring in public education. Within this venue, verbosity is frowned upon and brevity is preferred. When responding to a question, it was necessary that I give a very simple response, yet provide sufficient detail to facilitate understanding. The necessity for simplicity was not a reflection of the Board's intellect, but an attempt to package concepts so others could become ambassadors for public education.

The Forensic Leader has the knowledge and understanding to act as substitute for any position within the organization and do well. At school I was expected to be able to explain to my staff how decisions made by federal, state and local governments would impact the district and them personally. Understanding the big picture is critical to explaining the impact at the district level. At the same time, I needed to be able to train custodians how to clean a toilet, or to mop, strip and wax a floor after I had compared the prices and quality of products from four different sales representatives and placed an order for products. Serving as the leader of a school requires one to understand how students are performing individually as well as how they compare with one another, with students in comparable school districts, and with their peers on the state, national and global level. Within data analysis lies an inherent expectation that leaders comprehend the data and use it to draw conclusions and make predictions for the future success and failure of students. Based upon these predictions, the leader is responsible for insuring a plan of remediation for struggling learners while simultaneously challenging students who have mastered the content. When student performance is not where it should be, the leader is held accountable. If today's educational leaders do not understand how education is delivered in other districts, as well as on state, national and global levels, they are already at a distinct disadvantage.

In our spare time, when we are not breaking up or investigating a fight, consoling a teacher due to the loss of a loved one, reading divorce papers to see if a father can check out his child without the ex-wife's permission, stopping a bloody nose, feeding lunch to 712 students within two hours, or getting these same students to class punctually and safely, we are attending meetings. These examples provide a glimpse into the life of a good school administrator and attempt to further understanding of the requirements for a forensic leader at that level.

I recently had the opportunity to watch the television show, "Undercover Boss". The show sets up a situation where a company's president can disguise him or herself and go undercover to gain a better understanding of the company's organization at the lowest level. In this setting, the CEO of the company will do the mundane tasks that his or her employees are required to do on a daily basis. At the conclusion of every episode, bosses would return to their positions with ideas to better manage the organization, or streamline paperwork or procedures, or to implement changes to make the company better for employees who directly provided the product or service. "Undercover Boss" conveys to its viewers the need for a forensic leader. With Forensic Leadership there would be no need for an "Undercover Boss". Embedded in forensic leadership is the idea that leaders already understand their organizations at each level and so are able to perform tasks required at each level. Otherwise, a leader's decisions would be limited by his lack of knowledge of the organization at every level.

I had a number of valuable experiences prior to becoming a school administrator. I had the privilege of beginning my work experience as a school custodian during the summer of my junior year in high school. Working as a member of the summer custodial staff was a learning experience of its own. During this time I assisted with building sidewalks, cleaning bathrooms, and painting, stripping and waxing floors. After graduating from college, my initial position involved serving as a paraprofessional in an 8th grade math and language arts class. This was a very humbling educational experience; the most striking memory from that time was the lack of value some of the certified staff placed on the paraprofessionals in their classrooms. Following that experience, I was hired as a classroom teacher, and then as an administrator at various levels. These experiences provided me with the opportunity to understand and analyze the school system from the bottom up. My career appeared to be on a five-year cycle, with career changes occurring at those intervals. Although each learning opportunity was daunting, each was rewarding and helpful in preparing me for success in the next step of my journey. Even though every career move was not required for success, serving in many positions gave me a deeper understating of the jobs.

One example of forensic leadership is provided by the CEO of the Board of Directors for Southwire Company. When Roy Richards, Jr. took over as head of the company from his father, he quickly realized that to continue the tradition of success started by his father, he had to create a corporate image and compete nationally as well as globally. He also realized that it was important for his organization to convey that it valued its employees and wanted to invest in them. Mr. Richards having worked in the factory as a young man afforded him a richer understanding of the family's business, thus equipping him to lead forensically.

One of the changes made by Mr. Richards was to create a training center to ensure that employees were trained appropriately. He could envision the dividends that would bring in quality and consistency of product, safety, and retention of employees. Companies such as Southwire see the importance of investing in their employees and understand how that can yield huge dividends for the company. They also understand that healthcare costs are escalating and that employees are concerned about taking care of themselves and their families. Companies know they can better retain employees who are provided with good healthcare and that healthy employees can produce a consistently better product. As Mr. Richards began to fully understand this issue at its lowest level as well as at a leadership level, he decided to hire an in-house medical staff and pharmacist to significantly reduce his total healthcare costs and provide first class services to his employees at a fraction of the original cost. Forensic leadership involves identifying a need, understanding how the need impacts the organization, and creating a leadership plan that expands systemically until it reaches the lowest denominator. Roy Richards's leadership is an excellent example of a Forensic Leader. Southwire's medical center is the result of a forensic leader identifying a problem and designing a solution that extends systemically and allows the organization to reach its common goals.

Dear Mr. North,

Thank you for the tireless energy and keen vision you have consistently demonstrated the fifteen years I have known you. All of our students have reaped from the seeds of your leadership (including my two). Administration, faculty, and staff have grown as a result of your guidance and friendship. Personally, I am a better teacher and person because of your influence in my life. Thank you for allowing me the space to become a teacher without "putting me out" when you were "put-out!" You have been our roots and our wings!

The sweetest moment I remember is you showing up the morning after Alecia was born saying, "I've just held the first female President of the United States." You were the proud daddy. That said everything.

Thank you for guiding us through tough issues: poverty, inequity, curriculum roll-out, racism. Your gentle wisdom and strength has made this school powerful.

Charlotte, North Carolina

Chapter 3

CREATING A WELCOMING ETHOS

Trent,

Where do I begin? Finally after 16 years of teaching we were able to work together at CMS! Thank you so much for asking me to join this staff of awesome and dedicated adults! It is amazing to me how you were able to find "the best" from the cafeteria workers to the custodial staff! Everyone in this building is dedicated to the good of children! A quote from my favorite movie, "Remember the Titans", says it all—"Attitude reflects leadership." We have had an awesome role model as our leader! Always with a positive attitude and a laugh to share! These five years have been the best!

I am so happy for your new position in our system! As a graduate of this school system I know your goal is to make it the best system in the country. I know for a fact CMS has been the best! I have loved every minute here! When deciding what to do, as far as teaching, my grandmother told me, "Find a job you love and you will never have to work a day in your life." I have truly loved my job here, therefore, I didn't dread work nor was I angry at the end of the day! Thanks for making it great! I hope and pray you will love your new position!

From "Friendliest Female" to "Friendliest Male" Class of '86—

Good luck and I love you!

Miami, Florida

My first mission as principal was the establishment of a welcoming ethos for the middle school; it is impossible to have a successful program without one. A welcoming ethos encompasses the entire school environment and creates surroundings where people want to go to work, employees enjoy working together, parents feel safe and positive leaving their children, and students are excited about attending school. Driven and relentless, I embarked on the first task: designing the framework for a welcoming ethos in school.

Anthropologists have defined ethos as the *distinctive spirit* of a culture or era in history. The reality is that every school, system, or organization possesses a distinctive spirit known as an ethos, and it can be either welcoming or unwelcoming. I was about to open a new school that was partially formed from one reputed to possess an unwelcoming ethos. We needed to transform the culture and do so quickly and thoroughly. It is important to note that compared with many schools and based on traditional standards, this was a "good school". Unfortunately, the merely good school had become the expected norm for educational settings throughout our country.

Creating a welcoming ethos is a daunting yet necessary task. Organizations and businesses within the private sector spend millions each year to successfully create and improve their ethos. Reflect on your own shopping experiences. When you walk into a particular store you may be welcomed by smiling employees, hear music playing softly in the background, see pleasant colors and designs, and view a display of bargain items. What many may be unaware of is that all these things are intentionally created, based upon psychological research, to establish an ethos specifically designed to get customers in the mood to spend money. The concept is very simple. Stores do not want customers focused on negative things such as how much money they may have to spend, how long it will take to shop, or other pressing tasks ahead. Those factors can impact a company's bottom line. Therefore, everything you subconsciously see, hear, feel, and sometimes taste, are specifically calculated to relax your mind. The arrangement of products and layout of the store all form a well-designed environment used to create the ethos that will motivate you to go down a certain aisle and to purchase certain products. The business environment is specifically designed to fulfill its mission, from greeters at the multiple entrances of a Wal-Mart store to the polished and smiling receptionist at a local law firm. All are fostering a welcoming ethos that has been proven to work in the private sector, but was yet to permeate government entities, school systems and some businesses.

Who is responsible for establishing a welcoming ethos? This job rests with the individual who possesses decision-making responsibility. In public education, it is the school board and superintendent for the system and the principal for each school. I want to stress the importance of understanding that the principal or building leader personally sets the ethos for the school. The principal must *own* this responsibility. It requires targeted work and perseverance at the forensic level. A major portion of a school's success depends on whether or not the ethos is welcoming; the school leader must set the tone. It is also important to note that one person or an isolated event can reverse the work of an entire organization. The first task is to have an open and candid conversation about creating a welcoming ethos, which implies that one does not exist. Please be forewarned that this can cause a defensive posture so it must be approached honestly and in a non-threatening manner.

At our initial faculty meeting I addressed the faculty by making this statement: "As the principal of the middle school, I need your help. I need all of you to work with me to create a welcoming ethos for our school." The room became noticeably silent. After all, we worked in an educational environment—there is no one more nurturing or caring than educators. Of course we were welcoming! I did not choose to give examples at that time of what we were doing wrong. I am convinced that the discovery method yields more long lasting results. I desired instead to help the staff discover the concept. Once revealed, each staff member can see for oneself and the learning is never lost.

Many of the staff struggled with the discernible differences between a welcoming and unwelcoming ethos, and as I helped them understand the difference, I provided the following example: Imagine walking into an upscale boutique or department store: stiff smiles, cold environment, feeling you are underdressed, and being looked down upon. What are the chances of you spending money at the boutique? Remember visiting a relative or friend for the first time. Upon entering the home, prior to the host specifically saying "welcome to my home," an individual can sense whether or not he is welcome. The mat and décor at the front door, the tone of the doorbell, the texture of the carpet and color of paint chosen for the house, and more specifically the verbal and non-verbal interaction that occurs once you enter the home all set the ethos for the visitor. The host may actually be pleased about your visit, but before you can sit down your spouse may lean over and whisper, "I hope we are not staying long." Even though the intention may be to welcome, the guest may not sense that from their initial impression. Can you recall a time when you visited a friend or a co-worker and you were uncomfortable asking to use the rest room or requesting a glass of water? Think about it for a moment. No one told you that you could not have a glass of water nor were you denied the right to use the restroom. Even though you knew your request would be granted, something convinced you that they were not comfortable saying yes. That something is the distinctive spirit of the house. On the other hand, if the ethos is welcoming, one does not feel that it is necessary to ask if he can go to the restroom; He can say instead, "Can you tell me where your restroom is?", because you know it is permissible to go and use the restroom.

In education, we have the same ability to establish a welcoming ethos. The process begins with the principal and moves to other leadership personnel and then to faculty and staff. I had two assistant administrators and after a three day summer retreat, we were ready to educate and equip the staff with the ability to see and feel the invisible distinctive spirit which ensures that everyone who enters the building is welcome. Changing the tradition of flawed learned behavior required altering ideology. Together the faculty and I embarked upon a mission to change our ethos to a welcoming one.

Over the course of my tenure at the middle school, we read a variety of literary resources aimed at addressing the intangible elements of a welcoming ethos. To accomplish the task I turned to some of my favorite authors to assist us. The first book used in Year 1 was <u>Faithful Over a Few Things</u> by Dr. George O. McCalep, Jr., Ph.D. I strongly encourage organizations desiring to change their culture to consider beginning with this book. Because the book was written specifically for a church, I did not purchase a copy for my entire staff. However, I did devote a significant amount of time during the first year referencing the book, specifically Chapter I, "Cherish and Prioritize Relationships". Chapter I did an excellent job defining the five stages of relationships and informing the reader how to build relationships, an important factor when there is a need to make difficult decisions. The faculty had to understand, respect, and support one another. Because this was critically important as a new school, we spent a great deal of time the first year building relationships within the faculty, facilitating respect among the staff, encouraging them to value the strengths in each other, expecting them to always speak positively about each other and support one another. Before we could genuinely welcome others, we had to welcome each another. Building true collegiality and a more professional working environment does not occur overnight, and it was important for the organization to dedicate as much time and energy as was needed to accomplish this important task.

During the second year faculty study groups read <u>The Fred Factor</u> by Marc Sanborne. <u>The Fred Factor</u> deals with intentionally going above the call of duty. For example, even though everyone is not the receptionist, if an individual is in need of assistance, you assume that role. I wanted the middle school to defy the *Pareto principle* or 20/ 80 rule and wanted to create at a minimum, the reverse. During Year 3 the staff read the <u>The Difference Maker</u> by John Maxwell in faculty study groups. This book provided individual guidance for our personal attitudes. As an organization, our philosophy quickly became: 'We check our attitudes at the door prior to entering the building'. We were committed to not bringing our personal problems to work with us. All of our customers including tax payers, the Board of Education, our co-workers, our parents, and most importantly, our students deserve our best every day. The following year we read John Maxwell's <u>Leadership 101</u>. Now that we were mastering the concepts, we needed more leaders helping to cultivate and enforce it. The following year as the economy was struggling and we needed to ensure that our ethos remained the same, we read <u>Who Moved My Cheese?</u> by Spencer Johnson and <u>High Five</u> by Ken Blanchard and Sheldon Bowles. We could not allow the current economy to reduce the quality of education our students received. <u>High Five</u> focused on the philosophy of working together and winning together. As federal and state dollars continued to be reduced, it was essential for the staff to pull together and continue the tradition to which our students and parents had become accustomed. During Year 6 we read John Maxwell's <u>The Seventeen Indisputable Laws of Teamwork</u>. The resources allowed us to continue perfecting our welcoming ethos while developing more leaders and ambassadors in our building.

Creating a welcoming ethos requires time and commitment. With reading assignments, candid discussion and constant honest feedback and support, the ethos was changing, and by the end of the first year, it was much more welcoming. The reading assignments and conversation alone were not sufficient. The leadership staff and I had to model for the staff how to ensure that every individual felt welcome, that we conveyed the staffs' value and never resorted to insults or sarcasm. For the staff to make parents and students feel welcome, it was important for the leadership team and me to convey to the staff that they were welcome, valued, and that I was thankful to have them working for and with me. It is the principal's job to guarantee that teachers, paraprofessionals, custodians, cafeteria staff and anyone who works within our buildings feel welcome. I went to great lengths to make sure that happened.

As stated previously, this concept is not new. Retail businesses and others have been creating a welcoming ethos for decades and modeling it for their employees. Government leaders had to dismiss the notion that while it is permissible for the private sector to convey a sense of welcome and appreciation to staff with, luncheons or celebrations, it is unnecessary for the government sector to do so.

Tanner Medical Center, a regional hospital in Georgia, takes pride in being recognized among the top 100 hospitals in the country. The hospital leadership has worked hard to create an organization where employees enjoy their jobs and value their role in the healing process, whatever that role may be. The organization also recognizes that having happy employees benefits those who are more positive and more excited about coming to work. What a noble idea! My godmother worked at one of the major banks in town and the company employed similar concepts and ideas that made certain their employees felt welcome and valued. Even though her compensation was respectable, she was provided with a reward that she would have been unable to provide for herself.

As the leader of an organization attempting to establish a welcoming ethos, I decided to create an appreciative work environment at my school. I strongly believe that employees in the private sector work hard and deserve to celebrate and receive recognition. However, I am not convinced that the private sector works any harder than the average teacher or employee within the public sector. It must be noted that the staff was working hard and averaging approximately 80 hours a week, unsolicited. The custodians often had to ask teachers to leave at the end of the evening shift so they could secure the building, and the building was open at teacher request almost every weekend. For many government leaders who support the belief that working for the public sector is not as respectable or valued because taxpayers are paying for it will require an ideological change. Many citizens believe that it is inappropriate and unnecessary that we covey our value to government employees. In education specifically, leaders cannot subscribe to that ideology. Only the very best is acceptable for those who prepare our future workers, inventors, scientists, CEO's and leaders. Equally as important is public education's role in continuing the great democracy the free world depends upon; I believe that democracy without an educated population is a precursor to an impoverished and uncivilized society. Education is the best defense against weapons of mass destruction; therefore, leaders should hire the most qualified employees. Creating and maintaining a welcoming ethos is important to ensure the highest quality of instructors.

At the beginning of the Year 1, I began creating a welcoming ethos with something small. My administrative team and I spent over 1,000 combined hours preparing for the first meeting. As a new school, we did not have access to much money, but I was able to purchase a gift for everyone who worked for me. This was a tradition I continued throughout my tenure. In addition to the gifts, I provided the staff with personalized business cards and a genuine leather calendar/planner. I also provided a hot breakfast the first morning. However, what they seemed to enjoy as much as the gifts was the service they received on the third day of preplanning. This was a very hectic day as they prepared for the evening open house. I knew that many teachers also struggled to arrange for their own children while preparing their classrooms for a successful open house. In an effort to release outside tension for staff and allow uninterrupted time to work in their classrooms, I provided breakfast, lunch and heavy hors d'oeuvres for the school team. It is amazing how those three simple acts helped employees feel welcome and supported, and it was rewarding to see how teachers reciprocated by conveying that same sense of appreciation to students and parents.

It didn't stop there. What was provided for the staff during pre-planning was just the beginning, and minute in comparison with what occurred for the remainder of the year. I know that many schools and organizations place small gifts in mailboxes throughout the year to boost morale or to say "Thank you and I appreciate all the work you're doing". We did that as well. We also knew the winter holidays can be a difficult time for families, friends, and loved ones. As an organization, we never know how people are responding to what can be a stressful time and I did not want that stress in my building. During the winter celebration, my administrative staff and I went to great lengths to celebrate with our staff. We prepared a holiday dinner celebration for the entire staff along with another gift. In addition to our normal duties, the production began months in advance as we developed a theme for the celebration that I wanted to have a lasting impact on the staff. The first year's celebration was about fellowship and appreciation, so the leadership team prepared a traditional southern dinner with all the trimmings. Truly a feast fit for a king! There was also plenty for the faculty to take home. Not only did the administrative team prepare the meal, but we served it as well. The faculty enjoyed the special meal and looked forward to the special treat each year.

At the end of year one, we celebrated meeting AYP, the many accomplishments throughout the year and no longer having the lowest performing grades in the system. Creating a welcoming ethos was working and having a positive impact on student achievement, employee morale and community relationships.

For year two, the second winter celebration, in keeping with the prior year, we replicated dinner for the employees. To build up the excitement, in October I began to build teacher anticipation and excitement. I would say, "I hope you enjoyed last year's celebration because this year's is much better!", and the staff would become excited anticipating what to expect during the winter celebration. To build upon excitement (and being the great agitator that I am!), I would drop hints on the morning broadcast. For instance, I would say things such as: "I'm not sure what this year's winter celebration will be like but I do know that riding a bus is involved." And I had several teachers who didn't particularly care for riding a bus ask questions like, "What are we going to do?", "How far do we have to go?", "I know it's going to be exciting but I can't ride the bus immediately after eating and the food is always good, so I want to eat as much as I want." So, I would come on the broadcast three days later and say, "I can't tell you how far we are going or how long we will be on the bus, but what I can tell you is that you need to wrap up because it's going to be cold." And then I would wait a couple days and drop another hint such as, "For this excursion you will want to wear your blue jeans and tennis shoes because I can assure you that you will want to be comfortable."

The celebration that year not only included dinner, but I reserved a local theater solely for our staff and provided our own version of "dinner and a movie". When the bus pulled up to the front of the school, and the teachers walked out to get on the bus, we could see the excitement and curiosity on their faces. Prior to arriving at the theater, the bus took them on a couple of diversionary excursions to heighten the suspense. Once we arrived at the local theater, the staff received free popcorn, candy, and drinks. The movie the faculty watched was "This Christmas", a culturally enriching movie with great humor. Having previewed the movie, I knew my staff would not only enjoy it, but learn from it in the process. I worked with the theater's owner to keep the movie so that my teachers could watch it, as it was due to end several days prior. They loved the event, and they referenced the movie for several years. As you can imagine, the teachers went home for Christmas very elated and excited, wondering what I would come up with the following year to top this event.

For Year 3, the celebration had to exceed the prior year and it had to be very special. We were celebrating the receipt of the Governor's Gold Award, an award to recognize Georgia schools for making the greatest gains on the state standardized tests. We were the first school in our system to receive such an award. The winter celebration must be exceptional. Of course, the teachers wanted to see another special movie, but the perception of how educators spend their funds nixed going to the movies two years in a row. Plus, we could do better than that. After all, we want their performance to continue increasing.

In October the production aimed at maintaining the ethos that our community, and system expected at the middle school had begun again. As always, I used the morning broadcast to tease the curiosity of teachers, reminding them that the leadership staff was once again working on the winter celebration, reminding them that this would be a special celebration that they would enjoy. The staff would try to anticipate what we were going to do this year. We decided that in lieu of taking them to the movies and because they were our own "stars", that we would transform our media center into a temporary movie theater. Imagine a large media center darkened with black paper, with runway lights lining a red carpet, and teachers' names on golden stars as you enter. We had the bus pick up the staff once again. However, this time we took them around the front circle on the bus, brought them back to the media center, and walked them in on the red carpet (to our applause!) to see their names imprinted on the stars. We began the celebration that year thanking our "stars" for what they do for the children and parents and once again we watched a movie. The movie was chosen for its redeeming quality.

The winter celebration was important to maintaining the welcoming ethos at the middle school. However, celebrations did not occur only during the holiday season. Every professional development day that occurred at the middle school was designed similar to those offered in the business community, because we valued the teachers' time and wanted them to focus on whatever goals or objectives we had set for the school. At every Board of Directors meeting that I attend there is always food and fellowship to ensure that collegiality and camaraderie continues to be reinforced. I borrowed those concepts from the business community and embodied them in our professional development time at the middle school.

At the end of the year we always celebrated the success of the school year. If we had new faculty hired for the fall, we brought them in so that they could become a part of our faculty in the summer. They celebrated our success with us so they could anticipate contributing to our success the following year. We would have one of the premier restaurants in our community cater the end-of-the-year celebration, and we recognized our Teacher of the Year, so preparation of this celebration and the forensic attention to detail was evident.

The benefits of a welcoming ethos yielded tremendous dividends for our school. When our system went through SACS accreditation (Southern Association of Colleges and Schools), the accreditation team spent time in all of our schools. The Southern Association describes the accreditation process as a "set of rigorous protocols and research-based processes for evaluating an institution's organizational effectiveness. The accreditation examines the whole institution—the programs, the cultural context, the community of stakeholders—to determine how well the parts work together to meet the needs of the students." The team spoke very highly of all of the schools in our system, but they made special mention of the Middle School. The comment made by the committee was "You need to figure out what you are doing at the middle school and share it with the other schools."

In addition to the SACS accreditation visit, our special education department was audited after a focused self-study, and state special educators visited each school to provide feedback. The process is known as a focused monitoring. The team spent time at our elementary, middle, junior high and high schools as well as at the alternative school. They spent the least amount of time with the middle school, but their feedback indicated they were the most impressed with our school.

Our school system participated in a Georgia Assessment of Performance on School Standards (GAPS) analysis shortly after we had lost an associate principal, two teacher slots, a paraprofessional, and a secretary. Once again a committee of outside educators who visited all schools and facilitated the GAPS analysis conveyed how impressed they were with our school and our teachers' commitment to continuing success regardless of the tremendous reduction in staff during the budget process. Once again they raved about the middle school teachers and the ethos of the school (they also used the word), because teachers conveyed to them exactly what we were focused on.

Although the principal sets the ethos, the staff truly implements it. The school's welcoming ethos made it attractive to the best teachers. Hiring was made difficult by the number of quality teachers who wanted to join the staff. Every year I was principal except one, the system's Teacher of the Year was selected from my building. Due to our welcoming ethos, I was able to hire the best teachers, and I did not have to recruit them. We made our staff feel welcome and they rewarded us by doing an excellent job and ensuring that everyone who entered the building felt welcome. That is a powerful indictment on the quality of teachers hired and retained at the middle school. It was common for me to have parents whose adult children were new education graduates ask how their child could come to work at the middle school, but this time it was different. It wasn't because I was the token principal. Once this ball began rolling, it was almost impossible to stop it. We had implemented a welcoming ethos that yielded and supported the best teachers, and consequently the best academic performance. I knew it had nothing to do with me personally, but had everything to do with the principal and the leadership laying the foundation that conveyed to everyone that they were welcome.

In addition to reading and working with my teachers I needed to hire my own "greeter", as the first person in a school who interacts with the public is crucial. This individual sets the tone for what will occur throughout the visit. I recommended a certain individual as receptionist, and I knew that she was the perfect person to set the tone for visitors. She did so naturally, not requiring special training. Consequently she was loved by everyone and went overboard to make everyone feel welcome. I wanted someone who not only valued each ethnicity,—but loved life and people more. And even though my "Ms. Canada" annoyed me because she struggled saying "No" and found ways to say "Yes" even though I told her to say "No", it is important to understand that my receptionist was hired because she couldn't say

"No". She always went above and beyond in the interest of serving our public. An example: When a parent who was struggling came in wanting to meet with a teacher who was in class and could not be interrupted, the receptionist put herself in the parent's position and said "Ma'am you are not going to leave here and be upset. Please have a seat. You are going to see someone." She ensured that whether the parent met with the teacher or with me, that the mother was welcomed in our building and she left feeling better. And so that is what we have to do; we must hire good people, put them in the right place and allow them to do what they do best.

Dear Trent,

It has been an absolute pleasure working with you these past six years. I was in a difficult place back then and I truly believe this job saved me. Coming to CMS each morning gave me a sense of purpose, a place I could call my own. The best way to heal is to give and I am able to share love, joy and a sense of caring with the children here, my most favorite environment to be in. I greatly appreciate your confidence in me and for giving me an opportunity to try my best to make everyone who walks through these doors feel welcome. I have been at places where I have dreaded going to work. But I can honestly say that coming here each day fills me with much happiness. I appreciate your patience in getting over a few wardrobe bumps and for the thoughtful way in which you corrected mishaps. You created a relaxed atmosphere of closeness and fun while maintaining a standard of excellence. I love your analogy of making deposits first so that in the future withdrawals come willingly. I admire how you have used humor to calm many tense situations and I'm amazed in some cases when people leave laughing. That is a gift! I can't imagine a more giving, caring, understanding and fun-loving principal. Thank you for making CMS a home away from home for me and for everyone who invests their time here. I am so very grateful that I had you to ease me into the working world. I will <u>greatly</u> miss you!

Love,
Paris, France

Chapter 4

SETTING EXPECTATIONS

Trent,

It shouldn't have been a surprise to anyone that one day you would be moving on to a higher calling. Still, I don't mind saying that when it was announced you would be leaving CMS, it felt like the breath had been knocked out of me! It is hard to imagine a new captain of this ship. You birthed, nursed, and have been raising up our faculty (figuratively speaking of course) these past six years, and everyone knows our success is accredited to your outstanding leadership.

When I think back to that infamous interview day at West Georgia, I have to smile. You would ask me a question . . . I would answer. You would say "That's a good answer. Let me share with you something you want to add to your answer." From the moment we met, you started grooming me to work in your school system. I believe with all my heart that God's hand was in my employment here. You are a great principal. Little did I know, you would become so much more than that. You have been a great leader, brother in Christ, and friend. I have enjoyed our candid conversations and appreciate the way you have always valued my input. I have learned so much from you, and I will borrow lyrics from the musical "Wicked" to give you my biggest compliment . . .

> "Because I know you, I have been changed
> for the better . . .
> . . . because I know you, I have been
> changed for the good."

Oxford, England

The second major focus for a principal is establishing high expectations for the school, just as teachers set expectations for students within their classrooms. It was my responsibility as leader to not only set high expectations for my teachers, students, and parents but also to assist them in getting there. John Maxwell writes, "Leadership ability is the lid that determines a person's level of effectiveness." The weaker an individual's ability to lead, the less likely an organization will reach its potential. Conversely, the higher the level of leadership, the greater the chance the organization has to reach its potential. The organization's leader, for better or for worse, determines the potential of the organization to reach its highest level of effectiveness. Dr. Maxwell refers to this as "the law of the lid". Simply stated, a school can only achieve as high as its principal skill level. It is important that the principal understands that and continues to develop and strengthen his knowledge and skills. I am convinced that the quality of the classroom teacher has the greatest impact on student gains; however, I am equally convinced that the failure of a school and an organization is due to lack of leadership. The opposite would be true as well. When a school is successful, it is in part the result of strong and effective leadership.

The work required for leadership is very demanding in time, knowledge and development of relationships. The average workweek for an effective principal is approximately 80 plus hours a week, not including football games, parent teacher volunteer organization meetings, community events or school performances. The principal's work hours reflects the time required to meet federal, state, local, staff, parent, student and community expectations. One cannot set expectations without having a good work ethic. The leader must have a set of skills that are knowledge based and must be committed to gaining more knowledge.

If the principal has high expectations for the school's teachers, staff, parents, and students, ultimately, the staff will achieve them. So, I began a process of setting high expectations for the staff, and it was critically important for everyone to see me implementing those same expectations in the role of principal. The advice I received from prior leadership instructed me to sit back, lead from afar and direct the actions of everyone else. It sounded a lot like allowing your constituents to see you but not hear you. Are you familiar with the concept of being seen but not heard? I do not believe that is how you lead effectively. If I allowed the assistant principal who was primarily responsible for discipline to set the expectations for discipline and to implement her plan for discipline, then I would not be conveying an expectation as to how I want my students to be dealt with from a disciplinary stand-point. I also had an associate principal who was responsible for assisting me with curriculum. Once again, if I remained on the sidelines and allowed her to guide, direct or chart the path for curriculum, I would not be setting the expectation for curriculum development and implementation. I can apply this same concept to the custodians and the cleanliness of the building, to the way we managed our funds, as well as to how we interact with the community and our parents. I am saying that those who choose to lead in that manner will not be successful. Leaders must discover their own leadership style. However, I have observed many styles and the one that I believe works in any organization is Forensic Leadership. It would be difficult to have a successful organization with conflicting expectations. The best decision I made was follow my instincts, experiences and knowledge.

Originally, my style of leadership, Forensic Leadership, was a difficult concept for my leadership staff to accept because they were ready to lead and had many good ideas. To facilitate this process, during a meeting with the leadership staff I stated, "I am excited that you are a part of the middle school's leadership staff. I chose you because I value what you bring to the table and I know you will be an asset to the middle school. However, during this first year your contribution will not be as much as you would like. It is important that I not only set expectations for my teachers and parents but it is equally important that I clearly convey my expectations to you as the leadership staff as well. Once I do that, I can begin to hand it over to you." I shared my airplane analogy with the leadership team.

I have never flown an airplane before but my first year as a principal in a school is analogous to flying a plane. I want to sit in the captain's seat and monitor all the gauges prior to take off and make sure that the plane is ready to take off. When the traffic controller comes on and says, "Mr. North, you are cleared for takeoff", I want to fly the plane during takeoff and throughout the flight. When we hit turbulence I want to adjust by climbing higher in an attempt to fly above the turbulence or lower to fly below the turbulence or make the choice to fly around the turbulence. I want to land the plane. Then I want to replicate the process and bring the plane back home safely. During the flight I will model my process and convey my expectations. The following year I won't need to fly it because I will have flown before, and I will begin to hand over more responsibility to you. Yes, I know and I did many of these tasks as an assistant principal, so you ask, "What is the big deal?" I believe that sitting in the captain's seat is tremendously different than sitting in the co-captain's seat, and I need to be the captain." The leader needs to be able to fly the plane without a co-captain if necessary.

And so it is important for the principal to convey those expectations. For the first year that the middle school was open, I set the agenda for the curriculum team meetings. I would meet with my associate principal and I would dictate to her what I wanted to occur at the meeting. The process involved a dialogue and not a monologue, with the final decision reflecting my expectations. On one occasion, I was attempting to set my expectation for the amount of rigor required in a benchmark assessment to adequately prepare a student for the state's assessment. Benchmark assessments were new to our fourth and fifth grade teachers, and I wanted the benchmark assessments to be equally as rigorous as, if not more rigorous than, the state's benchmark assessments. Some teachers struggled with that concept. It would require classroom instructional time and this was a discussion for the principal to have with the staff. It was an easy decision: in order to exceed the state standards, the expectation must be greater than the state's. I am not sure that everyone embraced my logic. The state's benchmark assessment is mentally challenging and completely drains our children. It's like taking a child on Monday and telling them to run a lap. Upon completion, one says "Good job. Go home." Then each day of the week you instruct them: "Run another lap. Good job. Go home. "On the day prior to the assessment you tell them, "Now, when you get home we don't want you to run a lap; we want you to run in place for at least five minutes." Finally, the day of the big assessment is here that is going to determine teachers' careers, and decide whether or not students can go from one grade level to the next, and we say, "Ok, we need you on the track. Now I need you to run a mile, and I need for you to run that mile within three minutes and fifty-nine seconds. I know you can do it. I really know you can do it because we have been working on this all year long. If you look at how many laps you have run and add them all up together you've probably run fifty miles, so make us proud." That is exactly what we do to children in education, and I was committed that would not occur at the middle school. When our students took the end of year assessment for the first time, the staff was nervous because the students used terms such as 'easy', 'not bad' or 'easier than our benchmark assessment and teachers were unsure how to interpret the students' responses. Several students noted the benchmark assessments helped them prepare, and they wondered why we did not have it in all subjects. Had I not been involved at the Forensic level, I would not have been in a position to ensure that my expectation was conveyed. I instructed the curriculum specialist to keep it at the same length and it was now clear why that was so important.

Another example for conveying expectations occurred in the area of discipline. During the first year I met with my assistant principal (AP) and was involved with many of the disciplinary decisions. We would have rich dialogue about how to motivate children to follow the middle school's five expectations. The expectations were simple: Be prepared, complete assignments, follow directions, respect yourself and others, and use appropriate manners in all areas of the school. The most important skills I wanted my AP to master were the ability to listen, get to the cause of the problem and hold the guilty party accountable. Sometimes, the guilty party was not the child but the teacher. The expectation was fairness for everyone. Being fair with everyone involved not assuming that children were the guilty party simply because they had been sent to the office. Once again, it was the principal's job to convey this expectation.

The last example of a forensic leader setting expectations involved the cleanliness of the building. I expected the building to be cleaned and remain clean. I could not simply tell the custodian that without specifically conveying my expectations. For me to tell the head custodian, "I want my building to be clean," not provide training and *inspect what I expected* would not yield the results that I wanted. I worked with my custodians on how to clean a bathroom and how to maintain that level of cleanliness which required that I know how to clean a bathroom. During one of my first conversations with my custodial supervisor, we were doing one of our regular tours of the building and there were black marks along the sides of the walls on several of the halls. I asked her what she was going to do about this. She responded, "Well, I'm going to put in a request for maintenance to have the building painted." We had an excellent maintenance department, yet I asked when she thought they would be able to paint it. Her response was, "Either Christmas break or summer break—and it must to be approved first." I asked, "Now what is my expectation of you?" She replied, "For me to keep the building clean." I asked her, "Have you ever painted before?" And she said "Yes." I said, "Do you have anyone on the custodian staff that can paint?" And she again replied, "Yes. The night supervisor paints for a living on the side." Then my question changed. "Why would you put in a request for maintenance when you have someone on staff that can do it for you?" That presented me with the opportunity to clarify my expectation: "It is my expectation that when a child puts marks on the wall, they come down within 24 hours. If he puts it up every day until we catch him, we should have the paint needed to take it down." When I returned to school on Monday, each hall of the building had been painted up to a certain level, and because the painter was experienced, he was able to blend the paint in without having to repaint the entire wall. This type of action occurred regularly in the building. From the superintendent to visitors, comments heard at the end of Year 1 were, "Wow, your building still looks brand new." Expectations! At the end of year two, "Your building still looks brand new." At the end of each of the next four years the comments continued, "How do you do it? Your building still looks brand new." It still looked new because it was the principal's expectation that the building be kept clean. Everyone who worked in the custodial department had to contribute to meeting that expectation. If I had not conveyed that expectation, when the bathrooms were messy they would not have been properly cleaned. Without that clearly conveyed expectation, they would have waited on someone else to paint. Without that expectation, the floors would not have stayed in immaculate condition. I never once told teachers that they could not hang things on the wall, or eat in their rooms, or track in dirt and mud from outside. I never once limited their use of the facilities yet always maintained the quality of the building.

Trent,

I want to tell you how lucky I was to be selected to come to CMS. It was definitely a surprise. I thought there would be no way I was leaving CES over Craig and Robin, but I am so happy that I got this opportunity. I have appreciated the trust you gave me to run a P.E. program the way I needed to and appreciate all the support you have given me. You have taught me a great deal about leadership. You have had a great vision for this school and have created a family atmosphere among the staff and students. That is a great accomplishment in a school setting and I have never been part of a school as a student or teacher that this atmosphere has existed more than here. I will miss all the conversations that we have had and all the wisdom you have provided me with. It was always great having the Monday afternoon lunch conversations on how each game played out the week before. This school has come a long way since that first year and at times we may have not been able to see the "big picture", but you did and you made this school great. You will be missed, but we will make sure this school stays "great" even after you leave.

Minneapolis, Minnesota

Chapter 5

Politically Savvy

Mr. North,

You are truly one of the most amazing people I have had the pleasure of meeting and getting to know. Commitment, conviction, courage, character, confidence, caring, and courtesy define your leadership.

Thank you for being a spiritual, serving, and available leader. I will miss you.

Who can find a faithful principal, for his price is far above that of a white board or even a Promethean.

The heart of his teachers doth safely trust in him whether he is with a school parent or a board member.

He tries to do the best for his faculty and staff as long as he lives.

He learns to use the tools of his trade and isn't afraid of a hard day's work.

He is knowledgeable about world affairs and uses this for his co-worker's enrichment.

He rises early in the morning for his devotions and asks for wisdom for his daily tasks.

He considers investments carefully and buys materials with an eye toward the future.

He watches his health and keeps the sort of diet he needs in order to stay physically fit.

His work is of good quality even if he has to put in extra hours to make it that way.

He is concerned about social issues and tries to help those who are in need.

He isn't afraid of difficult times, because he has done what he could to provide for his team.

He nourishes himself and his workers both physically and spiritually.

His teachers are well-thought-of in their community, because he never belittles them.

He is strong and honorable and is a happy person, easy to work for.

His conversation is wise and uplifting. In conflict he makes it a rule of his life to speak kindly.

He is interested in all things that concern his teachers and is neither lazy nor indifferent.

His staff loves him and admires him, and his teachers are proud of him and say,

"Many principals have succeeded in this world, but you are the best of them all."

Flattery is deceitful, and good looks are only on the surface, but a man who loves and fears God shall be truly praised.

This sort of principal deserves to be treated like a king; for his life proves that what he believes is real.

Farrah, Italy

Within society we often struggle with how to handle civil discord. As a result of that struggle, we are unable to perform at our highest level and by default may establish new inappropriate norms and stereotypes. The community that truly recognizes and values its differences will serve as the leader for the new millennium. This is where political savvy becomes a critically important element to forensic leadership.

Understanding the political environment and politics of the organization is vital to the success of any leader. Many rely on the leader for a productive work environment, job security, fairness and equitable opportunities within the organization. This expectation not only applies to private businesses but to all types of organizations. There is a misunderstanding in government and education in particular about the role politics should play in the workplace. As one of the most educated workforces in America, requiring the majority of its workforce to have at a minimum a four-year degree the educational profession is seen as the most politically naïve group of in some areas of our country workers.

As the leader of the middle school, it was my responsibility to have courageous conversations with my staff which at times included dialogue about public policy. Leaders must be politically knowledgeable when discussing public policy. The stakes are too high for leaders and educators who do not master the art of being politically confident and the consequences are dire. If one is inept in navigating the political system, not only do the adults, children, employees and community lose out, but the individual vested with responsibility loses as well.

As previously stated, when I received my appointment, blacks and whites, and to some degree the superintendent who recommended me struggled with different aspects of my appointment. The struggle is not uncommon and served to be a source of great motivation. I suppose that was to be expected. Despite the unfair complication that I was blessed with at birth, which reduces my chances of getting skin cancer, failure was not an option. When I realized that I could not change the culture of my building without having frank conversations about difficult topics such as gender, religion, region of the country, social economic status and race, I also knew I had to demonstrate confidence and savoir-faire in my approach. If I led the initial conversation, the response could be "here we go again with the Black issue." To ensure maximum participation, I worked with the system's chief academic officer and the director of student services to begin the dialogue with my staff. I know that many people may believe that color does not matter; however, I am convinced that as a black male it was politically savvy of me to begin the dialogue with two white females. Without their initial support, the conversations would not have been successful. Those two females had the perfect amount of melatonin and political capital within the organization to begin the dialogue. So during two days of post-planning prior to the summer of opening the new school, we began the discussion, and the two directors did not hold back. We started the discussion by talking about the disparities and inequities in education. At this point, it was not a conversation but a monologue. The faculty was initially perplexed by the data and not willing to take ownership individually or collectively. As the school leader, however, I was committed to seeing the task through.

When the teachers returned in the fall, I continued the conversation started by the directors. However, for the first couple of months, I used their names a lot and referenced their presentation on many occasions. While having courageous conversations off borrowed capital, I worked very hard to build my own political capital within the building. Consistency and correct decisions can increase political capital. The more difficult and challenging the situation, the more political capital one earns. One can only advance an organization so far on borrowed political capital.

As I have stated, leadership does not come with a title nor can it be bestowed upon an individual; it is earned. It can be defined by one's ability to motivate and get others to act. I had to make some difficult decisions early on which provided me with victories. With the newly gained capital, I began to have an increased number of necessary courageous conversations. I did not select the topics; however, when an opportunity presented itself, I seized the opportunity.

The need for candid, frank conversations did not exist only at my school, it existed in neighboring school systems and businesses throughout the state. Actually, I am confident that I could pick up the telephone and find similar situations throughout the nation. Many of my colleagues were struggling with issues of inequities occurring across multiple districts but were afraid to address the issue because of the potential political outcome. Since I was well known through neighboring counties, other leaders of all ethnicities would share their similar issues and concerns. The question before me and most leaders is simple; do we truly lead to ensure that equity is paramount throughout the organization, or do we continue with the status quo? Because failure was not an option, and I wanted the best for everyone in the organization, the status quo was not acceptable. I had to dive into this issue myself if all my students were going to be successful.

I knew the organization I was charged with leading was a true reflection of the images, stereotypes, and the norms that occurred outside the organization's walls. This knowledge cemented the need to continue the discussion started by the two directors, but at a more rapid pace. A key motivation was the belief that my work could potentially increase the number of adults who would learn to set aside prejudice and racist beliefs and practices. Creating an awareness of passive racism and the resulting impact was the first step.

My staff was a good group of educators who worked very hard to do what is best for their students. On the first day of school, I believe that every teacher wants every student to be successful. I would have been fine with my daughters being placed in almost any class in my building. Even though I had some of the best employees, many were unaware of their inappropriate treatment of children, just as I had been before my eyes were opened. After having been in education for seven years, it took a first grader to show me that some of my actions, though well intended, were wrong for children. I was blind to my actions and behaviors and vowed never to allow my lack of understanding to deprive any child of his opportunity for a fair and equitable education.

A first grader taught me a lesson that has drastically changed how I do business publicly and privately. At the time I was an assistant principal at the elementary school during year two of my administration. Prior to being an assistant principal I had dealt directly with over 3,000 students as a teacher, and I felt quite confident about my ability to be equitable in my relationships, as well as ensuring that quality instruction prevailed. This young man was in a self-contained behavior disorders class with about five other students. At this point in my career I was designated as the principal for the upper grades (3-5) and another assistant principal was assigned responsibility for grades K-2. Every now and then we would assist one another with the handling of discipline. On this particular day the assistant principal called on the radio seeking my assistance with an altercation in the BD (Behavior Disorders) classroom, and I went to his assistance. Two young students were wreaking havoc in the classroom and I assisted in removing both from the classroom. One young man was placed in time-out and the second individual was taken home. The student was so upset that I had to restrain him in the back seat of the car for his safety while he was driven home.

I remember it vividly because I knew of this child. I knew his mother and grandmother, where he lived and where he attended church. From my perspective I had ample background knowledge of this young man. As I restrained him in the back seat, he continued to tell me, "I didn't do anything, I didn't do anything!", and I said what many administrators might say, "I understand that, but you are still going home." We took him home and the distraught youngster told his mother, "Momma, I didn't do anything. It was the other boy. He was picking on me and they won't listen." This was the first incident. Two days later I received a similar call asking me to come once again and provide assistance. When I got to the other side of the building, it was the same two young men who were in an altercation. We did exactly what we had done the previous time. We placed one young man in time-out and the other was taken home. This time the young man I was restraining in the back seat became even more agitated because he knew his mother would dispense with punitive consequences when he was brought home again. I knew that his mother had attempted to alter his behavior on her end. This time as I restrained him he said, "I can't believe you're taking me home. I didn't *do* anything. It's him, not me. *You are just like the rest of them.* Nobody will listen to me."

I took offense to this young man's comment as he was saying that because I am black and my colleague was white that I was just like the white establishment. The student was implying that I was being unfair to him because he is an African-American and the other student involved was white. Up until this point in my career (and even a little bit longer) I thought I was "color-blind" and prided myself on not seeing color. I dispensed judgments and consequences based upon actions, not the color of an individual's skin. I remember thinking that this young man was not going to get far in life if he continued to blame White people for his decisions. I did not appreciate what he was saying because I was so proud that I was blind to the color of a person's skin. When we reached his home and I opened the car door, the young man took off running. He and I both knew what was waiting for him on the other side of the door. Because his caretaker was older, I caught up to the young man and took him to his grandmother.

On my way back to the school I asked my colleague, "Why is it that every time we go to break up an altercation between these two kids that one goes home and the other one just gets assigned to time-out?" My colleague shared something with me that made good sense, at least at that point. He said," The one we are taking home can control his behavior and the other student cannot." That resonated with me because I knew that equal treatment is not the same for everybody. Equal is unique to each individual's needs, and I was okay with that. I returned to work and continued with my duties as I had for the past several years in education. About three days later I received a call from a secretary stating that the BD teacher needed assistance in her classroom. This time the colleague that handled the discipline on the other side of the building was not present at school and I had to respond to the call.

As I reached the classroom I could see first-hand the destruction between the same two boys in the Behavior Disorders class. In keeping with tradition and maintaining what the administrator had previously done, I proceeded to escort the students out of the room. One was placed in time out and the other was taken to my office. As you can imagine, one went kicking and screaming while referring to me as a racist. He claimed that I was not fair just like everyone else and screamed from the top of his lungs as I was once again forced to restrain him. I just happened to run into the nurse as I was restraining him. The nurse said, "Is that Johnny?" I said that it was. She said, "Let me help you by giving him his medicine." We took him into her office and she administered his medicine, which acted as a sedative. I will never forget that moment. I just cuddled him until he calmed down. When he was calm, I timed him out and sent him back to class and he was fine. I quickly noticed that the other child did not require medication to help him control his behavior. I went to the records and pulled both students' Individual Educational Plans (IEPs). What I found by reading the psychological reports and behavior plans was that the student I had recently brought to my office was the one who had the true anger/ aggression issues and required additional modifications. My decisions bothered me and prevented me from sleeping at night for the first couple of nights because I knew that my handling had been an impediment to a child's education. I knew that I had normalized everyone as being the same. I then began to track for the next three to four months how I would have handled a situation prior to this incident and after it. What I concluded was this: One, I was doing damage to all children and African-American children in particular, and two, I had a separate expectation for kids who were African-American than I did for Whites. I was less trusting and harsher. Because I was so confident in not seeing color, I missed how differently my colleagues and I were treating kids of color. What I learned was there is no such thing as being "color-blind". The only question is whether or not we are able to honestly look at what we are doing.

As a leader, I needed my employees to join me in increasing the number of students who experienced genuine success. Extending the ladder of hope to all students and providing the chance to escape poverty required the work of many individuals. It would not occur unless I began to tackle the norms inside of the organization. Equally as important, as the daily custodian of the students that were in my care, it was unacceptable for any of my staff to directly or indirectly harm children.

I recall a conversation I had with one of my employees who expressed her displeasure with interracial dating and how she pities the children of interracial families. I could not believe it. She had no idea that she was speaking poorly of my beautiful, precious nieces and one of her co-workers. I knew that if individuals believed interracial dating was unacceptable that they would interact with their colleagues differently, as well as with the bi-racial children who entered their classrooms. As the leader of an organization, I could not allow fear to prevent the organization from having such discussions. I knew that I could not be in every meeting, and I needed more advocates for all our students, parents and colleagues. Having courageous conversations was vital to developing leaders and a caring community.

So, being politically savvy involves recognizing politically what an organization has to tackle in order for that organization to be successful and then knowing how to go about addressing the issue so as not to ostracize anyone in the process. Every political issue and social issue does not have to be addressed by every organization. There are political issues that have the potential to be an impediment to the success of an organization. Leaders must recognize these factors and create an environment where employees can come together through thoughtful facilitated dialogue to have courageous conversations about the issues.

As the leader of the school I knew that I needed assistance with moving this momentum in the right direction. Having built upon the capital of the Chief Academic Director and the Director of Student Services, it became important for me to now begin to lead authentically. I owed it to my employees so that they could begin to rely on and trust me in this movement, while at the same time, I knew that I needed ambassadors in my building to represent the masses. Administrators in most organizations or in management rarely represent the masses since they are often removed from the daily activities of their employees. I carefully selected two teachers to serve as co-chairs to assist me in leading this process. Both leaders were held in high regard by their fellow teachers and with me, and together we selected seven other participants to serve on the core team.

I knew that we could not be successful if the learning reflected training similar to the past, so I borrowed a chapter from corporate America on how their employees are trained. This is not intended to belittle the way in which educators develop employees. One change made to enhance teacher participation in the dialogue was the setting. This small change had the potential to transcend the learner's approach to the information. I needed to free the teachers to think differently.

One objective with the core team was to begin having a dialogue about our many differences. In that way we could learn to value and respect these differences without prejudging one another and ultimately impeding a child's chance for a better life. Another objective was to equip participants to be leaders, to think, to analyze, and to enable them to feel confident when making difficult decision. If they left thinking the way I think, then all I would have done was create followers. However, if they left being able to discern what is factual and what is not when watching or listening to the media, or when reading the local state or national newspaper, then I will have equipped ambassadors throughout my building.

I asked each teacher of the core team if she would be willing to volunteer to spend two days with me in the summer with no compensation. Each teacher agreed to participate in courageous conversations. Those two days were the start of the systemic change in culture for the middle school. On day one, we met at the middle school and boarded a school bus for the local hospital where they had an opportunity to meet the CEO and learn from some of their struggles. Prior to the hospital's new leadership, it had not been competitive and the inequities forced many potential customers to seek medical assistance outside the local area. With the new leadership's ability to make politically savvy decisions, the hospital now controls the local market and is competitive on a state and national level. Elements of forensic leadership aided in the growth of Tanner Medical Center.

The hospital prepared a breakfast for the staff and allowed us to meet in one of their training rooms. The hospital CEO's presentation, the breakfast, and the quality of the room set the perfect foundation for civil discourse to occur. After all, how often are teachers allowed to meet and spend quality time with a CEO? The change in setting made it possible for teachers to have rich and meaningful dialogue.

The group needed someone neutral to help facilitate the conversation. I chose Dr. Beverly Tatum as the initial guide. Her book, <u>Why Do All the Black Kids Sit Together in the Cafeteria?</u>, promoted structured dialogue for almost every topic which needed to be addressed about inequities. Each participant was given the task of reading the entire book. Also, each participant was assigned a chapter upon which they would lead and facilitate their discussion. Prior to the end of school, all participants had to email me their power point presentation.

The title and the first thirty pages can be challenging and intimidating, yet for many participants it actually forced the conversations to begin prior to day one. For example, one teacher shared her experience while reading the book sitting on the beach. She vividly remembers the looks and comments she received. Others shared stories of people questioning the reading assignment and whether it was needed at all. Teachers within the building were questioning the reading, and I could imagine the pillow talk at home. I know my wife and I discussed the book. The group was able to have dialogue on topics such as the complexity of one's identity; white privilege and whether or not it exists; quotas; affirmative action; whether the term Black, Negro or African-American was appropriate; whether people with melatonin similar to mine are Cuban, Latino, or Hispanic, just to name a few. When we began this dialogue, most participants were convinced that they were color blind, yet by the end of day one, the majority knew they were wrong in that assumption. No one is color blind.

At 11:45 a.m that same day, the bus picked us up from the hospital and transported the group to the Small Business Incubator where lunch was sponsored by a local business. During the working lunch, the director of the center explained the center's purpose. Of course, the conversation did not end once we got on the bus nor did it stop while we were waiting on lunch to be served. In addition to courageous conversations, sublimely the teachers were learning how their work impacts the community. By this time, the participants were engaged and enjoying themselves. Most important, they began to feel safe and to share their beliefs, experiences, fears, questions and concerns. We concluded Day One at the Small Business Incubator Center. The teachers loved the day and for the next two years the civil discourse continued and is ongoing.

Day two started off with a meeting at the local school in the media center. Breakfast was started and as the facilitator I recapped the prior day's experience. The teachers commented about how they couldn't sleep that night for pondering the prior discussions and how many shared their day and discussions with their significant others. We began to proceed with the presentations of chapter one, two, and three of the book "Why Do All the Black Kids Sit Together In the Cafeteria?" and the teachers continued to facilitate healthy conversations on topics. The teachers would connect the topics from the book to similar situations at school. I did not take long for the teachers to realize the lack of interaction with co-workers and students based on differences. I remember one of the teachers acknowledging that she had been in education for over of fifteen years but had never even given it a thought that she had never gone to lunch with anyone outside of her ethnicity.

If my views, perceptions and interactions with a group of people or a community stems from television, the radio, or a newspaper, I have greatly reduced my chances of being politically savvy. While it is important for leaders to be aware of what the media is communicating, they also understand that some media outlets have agendas as well. Having knowledge of this fact and wanting to ensure success for my students compelled me to take the teachers on a tour of the westside. My intent was not only to dispel the myths that are often associated with the less affluent side town, but to also provide teachers with a better understanding of the community.

At 11:30 a.m. of day two, the bus picked us up outside the middle school and we journeyed from the bus to the railroad crossing on the other side of town. One side of the railroad crossing is considered to be blue collar or to some degree an upscale community. It was very close to the University. The other side of the railroad tracks was considered to be the west part of town better known as what was once reported in the newspaper as "the jungle". And many who were employed within the community had still harbored some perceptions that this community was "the jungle". I instructed the bus to pull up to the railroad crossing and drop us off. As we walked from the railroad crossing through the first neighborhood, the teachers were amazed at the homes and the people sitting on their porches in front of their homes. These were middle class homes in good conditions. They were not government subsidize living. Then we came to the corner of the subdivision where there was a local barber shop. At the beauty shop was a young lady who was having her hair done. She was actually having her hair braided and the teachers were able to have conversations with the stylist and the young lady having her hair braided. The teachers were in awe that the braiding process would take in excess of three hours per hair-do. In addition to the amount of time, the teachers were also surprised at the amount of money that an individual paid to have her hair braided. We left the beauty shop, and they met the owners of P&D Barber Shop. It was important for them to know the owner because everyone in the Westside community knows all of the barber shops and the owners. We walked from the barber shop to a vacant building, and at this building I had instructed my custodians to set up tables and chairs for us so that we could eat and dine in the community. One of the local restaurant owners provided lunch for us. In addition to providing lunch, the owner stayed and had fellowship with us. In addition to the owner I had the director of the housing authority to come and dine with us along with one of her managers. I invited the wealthiest African-American in the community to come and dine with us as well. The process was to change a paradigm of what wealth looks like, as well as what poverty looks like. Throughout lunch a wealthy entrepreneur, who was an awesome polo player and has his own polo team, spoke with my staff and talked about the number of businesses that he owned, about his polo team, and about his many accomplishments. The teachers were very impressed because they were not aware of this individual, what he meant to the system, to the community and the state. After lunch we walked through the government projects which were located directly behind where lunch was provided. On the way to the government projects we stopped at the local Westside recreation center. While visiting the local center, we were able to interact with many of students who were participating in summer camp. The children were just in complete awe as they saw celebrities, their teachers, coming into their building and ran up to them giving them a hug. You could imagine the children's excitement seeing their teachers. One little boy asked a teacher "Are you lost? What are you doing here?" The students really enjoyed seeing their teachers in their community. When we left the center we toured the government housing and many of the teachers were shocked at how small and nice the apartments looked. Some apartments were less than 700 square feet in size. We continued to walk the entire half of the west side community and we concluded the rest of the tour by bus. On the way back from the trip we discussed what we noticed after lunch.

I pulled everyone in and I asked the question "How many fights have you seen on our tour?", and the answer was zero. I asked the question "How many gunshots have you heard on our tour?", and the answer was zero. I asked the question "How many drug sales have you seen?", and the answer was zero. And then I asked the question "At any point has anyone made you feel uncomfortable or nervous while you were here?", and everyone unanimously answered no. And of course I stated to them, "I assured the teachers that I did not call the residents to tell them we were coming so they would hide or be on their best behavior." On the way back I asked the staff "What did you learn today?" The learning was very powerful. It ranged from "I didn't realize that there were more home owners in the community than there was government housing" and one actually began doing a calculation and estimated that the government housing represented less than 5% of the homes on that side of town. Also, the ethnic make-up of subsidized housing did not reflect perceptions. The home visited was being rented by a white female with four children, and the housing complex consisted of over 60% of white or Hispanic tenants. They just assumed that the west side of town was African-American.

Being politically savvy is important. As a school we discussed state and local policy and how it would impact public education. We had frank conversations about money and how our decisions impact the budget. As the principal, whenever the school board would create a local policy I would always share that policy with the staff. If the policy had the potential to impact the school environment or the teachers personally, I would always read the policy and have discussions with my staff concerning how the policy would impact the work environment. The discussion was not intended to create opposition nor support; that was not my job. The objective was to foster an understanding of the policies and procedures in a manner that educated and informed. It did not stop there. Conversations occurred about state laws and guidelines, and federal guidelines and budget cuts as well. I wanted the teachers to become informed.

Political savvy is a necessary skill for a leader, and a Forensic Leader must be able to have intellectual conversations about substantive issues, such as advantages and disadvantages of a free market, or whether the market should be driven by the private sector or public sector, the role of the government within the free market, capitalism, socialism, communism, the constitution, the executive, judicial, and the legislative branches of government, the role the local economy plays in state, national and global economies, the role the global economy has on national, state and local economies, and our perceived freedom of speech. Understanding the system at such a level will allow one to challenge and grow its people and organization at levels unachieved by others.

Trent,

I'm not sure where to start. I will say that I'm going to miss you a great deal. I appreciate how you have challenged us—always assigning a new book to help us grow and become better individuals. I personally have grown as a person and as a teacher and it's because of you. I love how you love my daughter and I greatly appreciate all the support that you gave me in her adoption and with her medical needs.

Trent, you are a great man. I respect you and love you and wish the best for you. You were put on this planet for a purpose and you are fulfilling that. I'm thankful to God for putting us together (even though it was a little rocky at the beginning—Ha). I wish you much success. Come visit!

Savannah, Georgia

Chapter 6

Customers are Right

Dear Trent:

I am happy for your new position, but sad to see you leaving the hands-on educational environment of the middle school. As an Attorney/Guardian ad Litem *for* parents and children, it was always a joy to have a meeting in your school with you and your staff. I would say that your strength is helping to empower parents and children so that they feel involved in the educational process. I was never worried that parents would feel disrespected or patronized in a meeting at your school. I was also never concerned about children feeling that you, or your counselors, or your teachers did not care about them as people.

I feel that there is a shift in the system to focus on "already-successful-kids" that don't need encouragement and support rather than providing kids that are not so successful with encouragement and support. The ethos of the middle school under your direction as principal provided encouragement and support for parents and students. There is a reason that every school that you are involved with is successful. Hopefully, the system will take your skill set and ability to improve all of the schools in the system so that all parents and students feel empowered and involved in education. May God continue to bless you in all that you do.

Best regards,
Athens, Georgia

The parents are right. In order to have an effective school, a genuine partnership between parents and schools must exist, which requires a marked change from the behavior of the past. Schools can accomplish some tasks without having a good relationship with parents; however, in order to be the best, a genuine partnership is required.

When I began my career in education as a paraprofessional, I looked in complete awe and amazement at the relationship between parents and education. The relationship was one sided and public education dominated.

In my youth I worked as manager of a well-known fast food restaurant. There we were trained that the customer is always right. We learned very quickly why this concept was important. If we did not have our customers, the loss would have a direct impact on the hours we were paid to work. The basic principles of economics were learned at the age of 16. I have modified this training a little. My belief is the customer is always right unless factual evidence proves otherwise. In public education, it has been and to some degree still remains completely the opposite.

In the schools, we often held meetings pondering strategies to increase parent participation. Thousands of dollars were set aside for parent programs and activities. Every effort was made to communicate events to parents, but program after program, parental participation goals were unmet. What I quickly learned was that this trend was not isolated to the system in which I worked. Actually schools within my system had better parent-school-system relationships than most schools. Studies have shown that parents in most communities feel positive about their community school.

Also, most school leaders pride themselves on supporting the classroom teacher and supporting the establishment. This is the education's version of "upholding the party line". In many cases, we do so at the expense of children and at the expense of public education in general. This phenomenon is not isolated to education. It is seen in all levels of government, and has influenced the current national cry for transparency in government.

Mastering the content and being knowledgeable about the political system makes it easy for practitioners to justify, cover-up, or explain away wrongdoings. Please understand that this does not occur in large numbers. I would set the occurrence rate in most schools at approximately 10%. This means that a thorough job of accurately identifying the problem and finding the correct solution is done about 90% of the time, and the school/system is being forthright with the community and parents. I am convinced that of the remaining 10 percent, only half of the time has there been a deliberate mistake and cover-up by the school; the other half represents honest mistakes on the part of school personnel. Before anyone overacts, I need to put all of this into perspective. In just about any other situation, 90% average would be considered a favorable number. There is not a public official alive who would not like a 90% approval rating. Most important of all, it must be understood that most educators do not go to work with the intent of manipulating students. The problem with the 10 percent error rate is that in many cases the parents share their negative experiences at church, soccer practice, tennis practice or a football game. This can quickly become an indicator of the norm for many parents and community members.

Many of us participate in some type of cover-up whether we are willing to admit it or not. In the United States, as true patriots, we believe our country can do no wrong when dealing with foreign countries, yet in many parts of the world the belief is that we can do very little correct. You may be seen as unpatriotic if you do not support what our country is doing, whether it is right or wrong. Even though I know cover-up occurs in government, the private sector cannot point its finger solely at the government. The fall of Enron, the collapse of the housing market, the Wall Street fiasco, church scandals, and the decline of the banking industry are examples of organizations that supported false numbers.

In order to foster a good parent and school partnership, we must change our approach to our customers. As the leader of the middle school, I set out to create a genuine partnership with my parents. It began with the premise that the parents are right. This is a very simple concept and is nothing unique, but this simple concept helped propel Wal-Mart to its position as a retail giant. When Wal-Mart first opened its doors, a customer could return any item and receive a full refund without proof that the item was even purchased at the store. It did not take long for word of that trust factor to spread. Embodying the concept that parents are right does not guarantee that a parent receives his or her way; however, a parent does deserve to be heard and taken seriously.

Another example comes from an experience I had with a credit card company. At one point someone obtained my credit card information on-line and charged merchandise to my card totaling $357. When I received a statement, I knew it was not my charge and I quickly called the credit card company. They did not tell me, "Well, Mr. North, we're not sure about that" or "We've got to do an investigation, and if we find out it is not your charge we will give you your money back" or question, "Where did you put your credit card? Who have you given your credit card number to?" They did not begin by interrogating me and making me feel as if I were irresponsible or had done something wrong. They immediately credited my account back and explained to me the process. Therefore I knew I was not responsible for the charge, and that once the money was replaced, we would get to the bottom of it. In my partnership with the Bank of America, the company did not assume that I was wrong. Bank of America gave me the benefit of the doubt. I employ that same concept with my parents.

The concept that parents are right was a difficult concept for my staff to embrace and for many of my colleagues across the state to embrace. Other administrators frowned at the idea and frankly, thought I was crazy. I could not get them to understand the importance of working with parents by beginning with the idea that the parents are right. I knew my teachers struggled with the idea as well. One afternoon when I was sitting in a parent-teacher conference, it came to a head with two of my teachers. We were meeting in the conference room and the seven individuals involved in the meeting were all seated around the conference table. The meeting consisted of a mother and father, an assistant principal, two teachers, the counselor and me. The parents asked for the meeting, so as the facilitator I allowed the parents to drive the meeting. The mother led the conversation and presented concern number one, "The teacher is mean to my child and always picks my child as an example of something negative". She also stated that when she e-mailed her child's teacher, the teacher never responded in a timely manner. She stated, "When I write in my child's journal, neither teacher communicates back with me. And last, I never receive work home in a timely manner." Now, if all of these things were occurring, the mother had valid concerns and had a right to be frustrated with our program. In lieu of trying to blame the child or become defensive, I immediately stepped in and said, "Ma'am, I apologize that there is a communication breakdown between you and the school. If we have done anything to help foster that, we are going to correct it, because we want your child to be successful." What I wanted to do next was allow my teachers an opportunity to share their classroom procedures. Good classroom procedures will address most parents' concerns without having to tell the parent that the child is the one in need of structured guidance. The goal is always the factual concern and not personalities. We want to address the problem at its most forensic level. As each teacher would explain her communication process, it was very clear that over a nine-week span, that one teacher had dropped the ball twice. Anyone in education knows that failing to follow classroom procedures twice does not have a direct impact on a child's performance. We also learned that the child wasn't taking things home the way he was supposed to. When we left the meeting the mom was excited: she had been heard, she felt valued, and we had a plan to move forward.

When the meeting was over the teachers told me they had been very nervous going into the meeting, and both said, "You know Mr. North, we were wondering whether or not you were going to support us in the meeting." My response to them was, "I will always support my employees. Supporting you is paramount to me because I am investing time, money, and energy into your success, but it is important for you to understand how I will support you. I will not support you at the expense of making a child look wrong. I will not support you at the expense of making a mom wrong when I know that we made a mistake, and you know that we erred. If we made a mistake, we will admit it, regroup and start the process over again. My support to you is that I do not expect you to be perfect. When you mess up, it won't be an automatic write-up in your folder. When you make a mistake, you will know that you will have my support to come up with a plan to fix the situation. Once you have the plan in place that will be the end of it." What this allowed me to do was free my teachers of worry, and word quickly spread about how Mr. North works with his parents and students. What was amazing was that I was able to keep parents happy and support my teachers at the same time. Listening to both allowed me to strengthen the middle school organization as a whole. Steven Covey calls this concept "the emotional bank account". We have to make deposits in relationships before we can make withdrawals. It does not matter what the child did in 4th grade, the 5th grade is a new year. We cannot start with a relationship where we left off the previous year. Mom is saying this year is going to be a better year, and the child hopefully is saying this year is going to be a better year. If we pick up with our consequences from the end of the previous year, that impedes upon our relationship. At the end of this meeting, we had taken the high road, and we did everything humanly possible to let the Mom know that she was right, while at the same time creating suggestions that hold her son more accountable and hold Mom more accountable for a better year this year.

To further strengthen the genuine partnership with parents, I had an open door policy, and for me parents were high on my priority list. I would convey to my secretary that my door is always open for my students, teachers, parents and superintendent. Regardless of the task I was working on, if one of the four stopped by, I would stop working on the task at hand and meet with the individual. When parents are upset, sometimes they can do and say irrational things, only to regret their words later. I know that when something happens with my child, I do not want to play games and wait 48 hours just because someone has to make an appointment. For parents, I made sure that if I was not immediately available, my assistant principal was. When parents came, I stopped everything and we did an immediate investigation so that we could solve that problem. That is what partners do. They try to accommodate one another instead of putting obstacles up between the two. That is the forensic part of leadership.

Dear Mr. North,

Congratulations on your well-deserved promotion! I know you are looking forward to the opportunity to make many more positive impacts in the lives of our children. I would like to express my heart felt gratitude to you for the special relationship you have developed with not only our shared student but with me. As an educator, you have the responsibility to help develop and encourage your students to become the best students they can be and I can honestly say that you and your staff have done that with my child.

You made a huge impact on my child by speaking to him by name and having personal conversations with him that may not have always involved a situation at school. You became not only his buddy but I am sure you were buddies to most of your other students as well. He developed so much respect for you because of that simple act and felt confident in knowing you would take care of him. I know many days he felt like school was his home away from home.

Also, thank you for listening to me as a parent and making me feel that my concerns and opinions about my child's needs mattered. You and your staff always made yourself available and many times made me feel like I was the only parent at that school that you had to meet with. There was never a time that I walked away from a meeting feeling like you did not want to be involved in making a difference in my child's future.

We will forever speak wonderful words about our time at CMS and the fabulous principal, teacher and friend we spent two very impressionable, fun years with. Again, congratulations Mr. North!

Carrollton, Gerogia

Chapter 7

RELATIONSHIPS

Trent,

I can't believe that you are leaving "me". We have been on this journey together for about eight years. We have laughed together and cried together. Where has all of the time gone? Although I am happy for you, I am sad for CMS. You have poured your heart and soul into this school and its success. That's why "your" teachers vow to do the same. Our time together has been rocky at times but I know that the good times outweigh the bad.

Thanks for all of the many times that I called or texted you and said I would be late. You never made me feel bad, yet you continued to stress the importance of being on time.

I appreciate all of the "Pow Wows" we had. I know that those fights pulled out the best in me, and my "anger" made me want to fight harder to achieve.

When I look back over the times when I needed you the most, you were there for me. (1) When I was very sick in the hospital and you showed up and showed out for me and my family. That was love. I remember that I was stressing about coming back to work early and you told me to take all of the time that I needed. That meant a lot to me. I was able to heal properly without worrying. Most importantly, you assisted with my surgery process. When I was nervous about my procedure and wasn't sure which doctor I should use, you encouraged me and made calls for me. After my successful procedure, you also checked on me and monitored what I was eating. That shows that you care.

You have been a wonderful boss and friend and I will miss you tremendously. Come back and see us some time.

Rome, Italy

A relationship can be defined as a connection or association between individuals or organizations. In many instances, relationships can be the difference maker in the success of an organization. Positive relationships are essential to getting hardworking individuals to compete, produce and perform at a level greater than that at which they are accustomed to performing.

Relationships may be described as complicated, time-consuming, complex, simple, good, bad, demanding, daunting, broken, short-lived, long-lasting and rewarding. Yet relationships are key to the success of any organization. Dr. George McCalep in his book Faithful over a Few Things simplified relationships by categorizing them into five development stages: the pre-existing stage, the first impression stage, the acquaintance stage, the maturing stage, and the tried and tested stage.

I made a list of as many of my friends, associates and acquaintances as possible and calculated where they would fall within the stages. I looked at my family photo album, K-12 school yearbooks, friends on *Facebook*, those denied friend status on *Facebook*, and names in my cell phone, school directory, Carroll County employee directory, and many other documents to get my baseline data.

After analyzing my data, I concluded that approximately 50% of the people I identified fell into the pre-existing stage. This list included people who considered themselves friends of mine because we sat in the same classroom or they read an article about me in the newspaper, had a grandchild who attended my school, voted for me while seeking a public office, worked with my mother and heard stories about my childhood upbringing, watched me play basketball or football or heard about my playing basketball or football. These are individuals who have never met me yet like me because of what they have heard, seen, or read or dislike me for the same reasons. The same applies to someone like President Obama. Very few have sat in the same room with the President, had a personal conversation with him, or been invited to the White House to have a meal with him. Yet because of the position he has and statements he has made, the data shows that he has formed good or bad relationships based solely upon Stage 1 criteria. The pre-existing stage is an important stage which provides an opportunity for the leader to expand his platform while exerting minimal effort. We can never underestimate the statement "your reputation precedes you.

The next stage is the first impression stage. This involves actually meeting an individual and another 5 percent of relationships don't make it beyond this stage. If someone makes an unfavorable first impression, you are unlikely to get to the point where you will sit down and have a meaningful conversation that allows you to move beyond this stage. About 5 percent of our relationships get stuck here. Usually if you can get past the first impression stage, you can get to a point where you start getting to know someone and can begin to foster a stronger relationship. If 50 percent of our relationships fail because they are pre-existing, and 5 percent fail because of first impressions, it is no wonder that the circle of influence in our personal lives is so small and our list of friends is so short.

Before we even enter into Stage 3 we have already eliminated approximately 55 percent of prospective relationships. How does the remaining 45 percent fare? Stage 3 is the acquaintance stage and approximately 30 percent of my relationships fell into this category. The acquaintance stage involves individuals who are getting to know one another. This happens as we learn what we like or dislike about a person as well as their perceived strengths and weaknesses, and they learn the same things about us. The acquaintance stage includes many of our colleagues, people we work with or with whom we attend church, people we speak with regularly and know well enough to ask about their families. It may include those who are actually extended family members we must interact with, but if we had a choice we wouldn't invite into our homes. Even though there is kinship, the relationship remains in Stage 3 and never matures beyond that.

Stage 4 is the maturing stage. For me, the maturing stage encompassed about 10% of my relationships. This group includes friends I may call to seek advice, individuals I have had heated arguments with, where we both can voice our opinions and still remain friends when the argument is over. This group of friends is not afraid to be honest with me, and I am not fearful to be honest with them. Our bond is stronger than the issues that may separate us at times. Because of this trust, we can have courageous conversations with and about each other and still remain close friends.

Stage 5 is the last stage and is the tried, tested, and proven stage. Only 5 percent of my identified list made it into this category. These friends are the individuals I could give a blank check if they were in need, knowing that they would not take advantage. They are the individuals I would feel comfortable having my children around. Even though we are the closest to this group, any member of this group still has the potential to act in such a way that they breach an organizational policy, a family value, or a church value. This group is commonly known as our inner circle.

Everyone references the importance of establishing relationships, yet we often fail to do a thorough job of establishing one. I must say that growing up in the projects as I did provided many with an innate ability to create relationships. My mother was keen at establishing relationships, and I saw that modeled in my life every day. My father was also very skilled at establishing relationships. If you take my less than affluent upbringing, which was centered on relationships and my parents' natural abilities to foster relationships, then you begin to understand why most people assume that I am a people person and that making and fostering relationships is easy for me. To some degree those assumptions are accurate; I did learn a lot from my subsidized living experience. Those who know me are quick to note that I always reference my government housing experience endearingly, because I wouldn't be where I am without that experience. My parents worked at two different companies, and they were the largest employers in our community. Being the oldest of my family also provided me with the opportunity to lead at a very young age. When my parents would leave for work, I would become the keeper of the home.

I would prepare breakfast and lunch for my siblings. To be sure that they could locate me if needed, I did not leave the house the majority of the summer my freshman year of high school. I was the keeper of the house from seven until three and all I did was watch television. I can remember only three channels—Channel 2, Channel 5, and Channel 11, each dependent on the weather and the precise location of the antenna on the roof. Even if cable was available, it was not in the budget. I was stuck watching soap operas all day.

Training would start at 12:00to get lunch ready for my siblings because at 12:30, **The Young and the Restless** was coming on and I could not miss it. Yes, I watched the soaps! At 1:00 I would watch **Days of Our Lives**, at 2:00 I would watch **Another World** and at 3:00 I would watch **Guiding Light**. Watching soap operas for me was the equivalent of a pilot training on a flight simulator. The relationships on soap opera series changed almost daily, and as I watched each show, I began to study the roles of the many characters. Once I learned each character, I began to study the writers. I became skilled at anticipating the writers' next moves, and I anticipated which options would be available. I became so masterful at it that I could tell you who was going to die based upon the subtle hints or lack thereof, so watching the soaps for me was not solely about who married whom. Believe it or not, watching the soaps afforded me an opportunity to understand synthetically how relationships occur and dissipate. I began to compare the dramas to what was occurring around me. Even though the television show was fictional, the similarities were very striking. Over time I learned the importance of relationships and the skills needed to foster and sustain genuine relationships.

As the principal of the new middle school, I had to model creating relationships with staff for my teachers; I knew that in order for my teachers to be successful, they had to establish strong relationships with their students. Rarely do people do what someone expects of them unless they know that someone respects and values what they bring to the table. It is important for leaders to understand that while people may respect and value a vision, mission and guiding principles, the work they produce is motivated by people. The leader must convey that he not only values the individual, but the idea of family as well.

With a staff of seventy and a student population of approximately seven hundred, it was the highest priority for me to establish relationships with staff and students. Each morning when I started my day, I would choose an end of the hall to start on. I would start on 4th grade hall and I would spend quality time prior to school with all of my teachers on 4th grade hall. I would start with, "Hello. How are you doing?" and as each teacher on the 4th grade hall approached me, I would ask a personal question such as, "How's your mother?", or "Tell me about your son/daughter." I would ask, "What's happening in your world?" I rarely discussed business prior to the start of school. I wanted to understand and be more supportive of my staff. I would listen intuitively, because if a red flag came up during the conversation, I would go back to that teacher during planning and follow up with the conversation. I would be there for them in a supportive manner. The following day I would go to a different hall and do the exact same thing. It would be on my calendar. I knew which teachers needed the most attention and which ones required the least amount. Based upon their needs I would regularly check up on them. What I quickly found was there was not enough time during the day to truly foster relationships. I then did something unthinkable in my profession and gave my cell phone number to everyone on my staff who wanted it.

Prior to this administrative position I did not have the need to text message. I was a little slow at first, but soon I had to call my cell phone provider and have unlimited texting added to my phone plan. Ninety-five percent of my teachers had my cell phone number and they called me in the mornings prior to school, they called me after work, they called me on Saturdays and Sundays, and they sent me text messages when they were struggling. I could be in the building working and even though teachers were not supposed to use cell phones during the day, some would send me a text message or call my cell phone if I did not respond promptly to an e-mail message on the computer. At first I struggled with my teachers calling me at work, and then I realized that administrators were provided with cellular phones to keep in contact at the system level because it was important, and I felt that it was equally important for my teachers to keep in contact with me. My relationships with my staff were genuine, and because of that I was able to be there for them and in return, we were able to tackle tough issues as a faculty such as differences in race, religion and politics. It also afforded me the opportunity to challenge them to grow more personally and professionally than they ever had before. I had the same expectation of their relationships with their students that I had of my relationships with them. I am not suggesting that leaders share their personal cell phone number with every employee; however, I am suggesting that a direct line of communication exists to allow all employees to have access to and a genuine relationship with an authority figure who can solve a problem.

I was riding in the car with a colleague as the two of us were returning from a training session in Savannah, Georgia. My cell phone rang as I was driving and she asked who was calling. I told her the name and she recognized it as a 4th grade teacher of mine. About five minutes later the phone rang again and this time it was one of my 5th grade teachers. My colleague asked, "You mean you allow them to have your personal cell phone number?" I said, "Not only do I allow them, I encourage them to call me." We expect teachers to be able to communicate with parents and we need to model that as principals. Establishing respectful relationships is absolutely essential.

In education, this idea is not new to teachers. It has long been the expectation for teachers to genuinely convey to students that they have their best interests at heart. Car salesmen understand this process. A car salesman may try to convince me how safe a car is, or how economical it is, or how much more mileage a car gets compared to another vehicle. It's the same concept. I do not know this stranger, and yet he wants me to take his word for it and it simply does not happen that way. The same thing occurs in education. I expected my teachers and my employees to know those they were responsible for, and I quickly realized that I needed to model that behavior for my teachers. I wanted my teachers to know every child in their classroom by name, to know their students' parents by name, to know where every child in their classroom lived. I expected my teachers to work diligently to genuinely understand the environment that each of their students came from, to know where it was, and to reach out to them. I know some are going to say that if you are at the elementary school level and you only have 30 students, that is not difficult to do. But what if you have 70 students or 120 students that you are seeing each day? I agree that the larger the number, the more difficult this is. Yet there are always those students who would benefit most from a relationship with their teacher, and teachers often can tell who these students are if they are intuitive and receptive to that idea. The best way to ensure that a relationship is not formed is to not expect one.

Finally, I had an open door policy for my students, parents and employees because I wanted my employees to have an open door policy for students and parents. My teachers and my boss could come in and demand a spot on my calendar immediately. It was important for me to have an open door policy for my parents, my teachers, and for that matter, my students as well.

Trent,

My student, my friend, my boss—
So many memories of our times together—cheesecake, Savannah, meetings, meetings, meetings, long talks, advice . . . .
I respect and admire you for always being there to listen. Time marches on and so will you; to greater things. I am so

proud of the man you have become (even if I still think of you as my student).

Our time together will be remembered fondly. Thank you for always making me feel like a "Master Teacher"!

May you find success and happiness in your future. Enjoy each day and keep that special smile. Thanks for a wonderful experience!

New York City, New York

Chapter 8

TRUST EVERYONE,
YET TRUST NO ONE

Trent,

Where to begin? The first words that came to my mind . . . THANK YOU! Thank you for allowing me to rediscover the "love" that I have for teaching! Coming to CMS everyday has not been a "job" but a pleasure. I was at a place in my teaching career that I was beginning to feel it was time for a career change. You gave me the opportunity to come "up the hill" to CMS and I rediscovered why I love teaching.

You have played the major role in making CMS such an amazing place to "work". You were instrumental in putting together the best administration, support staff, and teachers a person would want to be a part of!

I made a list of adjectives at the beginning of this "paragraph" to make myself not take up ten pages in this book.

TERRIFIC . . . You allowed me to join the CMS family from the very beginning, so that makes you "terrific" in my eyes. You inspire your teachers and students to also want to be "terrific". That is not an easy task! You have done a terrific job! THANK YOU.

RELIABLE . . . As my principal as well as my friend I know that I can rely on you to make sure the needs of my students are met. Our students rely on you to make sure their educational experience was second to none. I have been able to rely on your understanding and caring to help me survive the most difficult time in my life! For that I will be eternally grateful! THANK YOU!

EXCELLENT . . . Excellence follows you! You expect excellence in all that you do and it is contagious! Your colleagues and peers develop that desire for excellence after spending time with you! THANK YOU for leading me to find excellence in my life!

NURTURING . . . To our CMS family! At CMS we felt from the very beginning that we were a family. You nurtured our educational, personal, and spiritual growth as a school family! THANK YOU!

TRUSTWORTHY . . . parents, students, friends and colleagues all know that trustworthy is an adjective that goes hand in glove with Trent. I know that I have been able to sit in Mr. North's office and laugh, cry, and have very serious discussions and without a shadow of a doubt know that I was in a trusting environment. Parents and students at CMS are trusting with Mr. North to know that their educational needs WILL be met! THANK YOU!

THANK YOU Trent for stopping at CMS on your journey in your amazing life. I can say that I have been truly blessed to have been a part of your journey.

Our school system will continue to grow to be a system of excellence with you as one of our leaders.

So THANK YOU TRENT NORTH!

Venice, Italy

Being thrust into leadership at such a young age enabled me to make a number of preventable, yet costly mistakes. The most hurtful part is my strong belief that many people have been preparing me to make these mistakes my entire life, yet remains unaware of the need to prepare me and millions like me. Doesn't every parent want leadership roles for his child, every business for its leaders and employees, and each school board for its employees? I am convinced that in order for a leader in the new millennium to be successful and to foster a winning organization or school, leaders must master the concept of Trust Everyone, yet Trust No One. The concept is inherent in true forensic leadership. For leaders, Trust Everyone, yet Trust No One is applicable in any arena including government, education, the judicial system, religious institutions, personal relationships and race relations. The individuals and organizations that shaped my life have on many occasions, unintentionally misrepresented the concept of truth. Who teaches their children not to trust their family, the government, educators/teachers, and church leaders? After experiencing too many unintentional untruths that negatively impacted me, I adopted the principle "Trust Everyone, yet Trust No One."

When life was simpler, the need to redefine trust was not paramount. If the world stilled moved at the rate of <u>Leave it to Beaver</u> or <u>The Andy Griffith Show</u>, there might be no need to redefine the term truth.

You see, our systems of families, government, judicial, financial, political, educational, and religious institutions were all developed at a time when life was simpler and less complicated, when the risks were smaller, and when variables could be controlled in contrast to so many variables that are uncontrollable today. In order for today's leader to be successful, because of the complexity of today's decisions and all the changing variables that a leader has to contend with, one must learn to Trust Everyone, yet Trust No One.

The concept of Trust Everyone, Yet Trust No one began to formulate for me as a sophomore in college. I recall sitting in my Medieval Political Thought class at West Georgia College, as the University was known then. There were approximately 10 students in the class and one of my favorite professors, Dr. Wagner, was facilitating the discussions. At this particular time he had given the class an assignment to go home and read two chapters. We were reading about the trial of Socrates. On that particular day, I just happened not to have completed my homework. I was a sophomore in college and pretty confident. After all, many who started with me as freshmen did not return as sophomores. I was confident that I could maneuver my way through any assignment whether I was prepared for class or not.

On this particular day, we were all sitting around the conference table. Because our class was so small, we often sat around the co nference table for discussion, one could anticipate the questions and there was a lot of rich dialogue. Well, to start the class off, Dr. Wagner looked at me, and he asked me a question. He started, "Mr. North," (he always referred to me as "Mr." At the time, I didn't know whether it was out of respect or the mere fact that I was the only minority in the classroom, but by the time I ended the course I knew that it was out of respect for me). "Mr. North, are all laws just?". That was a question I wasn't anticipating. For a moment I had to stop, quickly take my brain back in time and try to answer that question. I quickly reflected back to my second grade teacher, a lady by the name of Mrs. Parkman. I remember her teaching the class, "The government is of the people, for the people, and by the people." She taught us that it is the government's job to protect us, to make sure that no harm comes to us and that we are a part of the government. And then I flashed back to my seventh grade Civics class, taught by Mrs. Rita Gentry. I remember her echoing a very similar comment. She also said the government is here to protect us. It is made up of representatives that are chosen by the people and that they represent us on the local level, on the state level, and on the national level. They would never cause harm to us. It is their job to make sure we are protected and that our economy grows.

The discussion was a bit richer than the elementary and middle school lessons. And so, I recalled my high school Government/

American History teacher, a Vietnam veteran whose name is nostalgic for many who attended Carrollton High School, Mr. Mike Lankford. He echoed what Mrs. Parkman had said. He echoed what Mrs. Gentry had said. But he put a military spin on it because he had served in the Vietnam War. I left there feeling very proud of our government, so when I answered the question I said, "Oh yes", very confidently, shoulders back, sitting upright in the chair with a smug smile on my face (as if to say, "Ha ha, no I didn't do my homework, but you're not getting me today, Dr. Wagner."), "Of course all laws are just. There is no way our government would create a law that is unjust." I am thinking to myself that if the government is for the people, by the people, there is no way laws could be unjust.

Dr. Wagner looked at me with a little smirk on his face, and said to me, "Well, Mr. North, if all laws are just, then was slavery just?" And just for a moment the room went completely silent. You could hear a pin drop. Not only did he fool me, but he fooled the nine other students in the class. What made this exchange so profound was not the mere fact that I did not know the answer, but that as an African American I was standing up for the system and the laws we are required to follow—the very same laws that we were required to follow at one time that had held my ancestors in captivity.

In order to respond to the question again, I had to take a different route to memory lane. As time stood still, I began to recall a time when I was probably eleven or twelve years old and was riding in the car with my father. We had a yellow Thunderbird with a moon-roof that leaked water. I recalled being stopped by the police, and I remembered the lesson taught to me by my dad during that traffic stop by a police officer. He told me, "Now son, here is what you do whenever you are being stopped by the police. Every move you make, you have to announce it to the police officer." He instructed me to watch. And I remember him saying, "Sir, I am reaching for my wallet. Sir, my hands are on the steering wheel, may I move them?" I remember him saying "Sir, I don't have any insurance", because at that time Georgia law did not require insurance. I remember him saying, "I am reaching into the dash to pull out my registration." At the time, I thought that everyone announced their movements when dealing with the law.

When I came back to the present, I had to say, "Dr. Wagner, you are correct, all laws are not just." In kindergarten through 12th grade we are taught to believe that all laws are just and that the government is good, that the government is here to protect us. We are taught that if we vote for the right city councilmen, county commissioners, school board members, representatives or congressmen they will represent us well. If you are a Republican, you can't trust the Democrats and if you are a Democrat, you cannot trust the Republicans. We are taught that voting for the right President makes us a part of the government and that our elected officials are going to enact laws that can only be right for us. We are taught to trust the system and you are considered unpatriotic if you do not believe in that ideology. Please understand me; it is my belief that we are to believe in our public officials, in our judicial system, in our criminal system, and in our leaders. I am convinced we have the best structure in the world; however, in order to make it better, we cannot give a blank check for trust to the system or to any political party. Even with our government, Trust Everyone, yet Trust No One.

It is our responsibility as leaders to recognize that there has to be inherent trust in our system and that there should be more trust than distrust, but as leaders, we must recognize the concept of Trusting Everyone, Yet Trusting No One.

The Trust concept applies to education as well. Nowhere is this concept more prevalent than in our public education system. Every year millions of parents drop their precious jewels off at a public or private school, entrusting that every school official has their best interests at heart, entrusting that teachers will do everything they can in order to make sure that each child receives the best education possible. Having been in education for twenty years, and having worked from kindergarten up to the high school level as an alternative school principal, an elementary school principal, and a middle school principal, the idea of writing a blank check of trust for public or private education contributes to one of the leading causes for child failure. Here is what happens. A child goes to school and subsequently gets into trouble. The child comes home and says, "Momma, I didn't do it. The teacher just picked me out." And the mother says, "Now, why would that teacher be picking on you? That teacher doesn't go to school to just pick on you." So the mom chooses to lash out at the child. You see, the mother or father has chosen to trust the teacher over the child. What parents really do not understand is that although teachers do not come to school to pick on any child, because they are human, just like pastors, religious leaders and many others, they bring their biases and their prejudices with them to school. They do not discriminate directly, at least not the majority of them. Sometimes it happens indirectly. Nevertheless, the number of times a student is redirected makes it difficult for teachers, or anyone, to handle every situation correctly and fairly.

For example, a junior high school teacher will interact with approximately 120 students daily. I would surmise that each student will be a part of at least three redirects. If the average students earn three redirects which could occur in the hall, between classes, on the way to lunch, at lunch, on the way from lunch or during the sixty minutes of intimate time shared during instruction, a teacher will make approximately 360 redirects daily, 1,800 weekly, 7,200 monthly and 64,800 annually. Based on the numbers of redirects alone, not to mention their own weaknesses and strengths, teachers and administrators will ultimately make mistakes. Kids receiving punishments for infractions not committed is allowed to occur only because parents have decided that public education is a sacred place and so must be given a blank check for trust.

Now, please understand me, the majority of teachers come to school for the sole purpose of helping every child; however when parents hold educators accountable, both child and school benefits. So even in the area of education, both public and private, parents need to embody the concept of Trust Everyone, Yet Trust No One. Issue no blank checks of trust.

Teachers are leaders and sometimes they don't realize the power they possess. Elementary school teachers provide leadership to anywhere from 18 to 28 students daily. An educator teaching at the junior high school level provides instruction for approximately 120 students daily. Teachers at the high school level teach approximately 100 more students, not including extracurricular activities. Teachers make the same mistake that parents make. If parents assume that all teachers are perfect and that everything they say is true, then teachers make exactly the same mistake with parents. They assume that the parents are reaching out to them because they genuinely want to work hand-in-hand with them to ensure their child's success. They assume that the parents want to work collaboratively with them because they want to support them, when in reality parents have their own agendas as well.

I remember when I first was appointed the principal at the Middle School, I shared this concept with my teachers. I told them to remember that the law specifies what conversations we can and cannot have with our parents, but in addition to the law, we have to remember that everyone who reaches out to us is not necessarily trying to be our friend. One parent was not pleased with the placement of her child, a common complaint, especially in the elementary school. The mom went to the teacher asking how her year was going and telling her what an awesome teacher she had heard she was. The teacher begins to open up, telling the mother what a challenging year this is going to be because she has multiple levels of students in the classroom. The teacher tells the mom that her child is very bright but that she is afraid she will struggle to challenge her child because she has so many different levels of students in the classroom that will be in need of additional assistance. At that point, this mom had just the ammunition she wanted. The mom left the classroom, came directly to the principal's office, and requested that her child be moved to another classroom. She explained that she did not like the demographics of the class and that the teacher had told her that she could not teach her child because there were too many different levels in the class. The teacher's conversation with the parent places the principal in a very difficult predicament. This was the first year opening the new school. The teacher had already admitted that she could not teach the child. Also, after a few days of looking at data, the teacher informed the parent that the child was above the other students in the class. None of those things were factual, but legally I could not share the test scores of the other students in the room. I had to move her child. When I look at my journal, on average I come across a minimum of ten conversations with parents where teachers have shared confidential information with them, and the teachers trust that it stays with them. It could be confidential information about another child or it could be confidential information about what is going on in the building. So, as leaders and teacher leaders we have got to embody the concept of Trust Everyone, yet trust No One.

Forensic Leaders do not write blank checks of trust. This concept applies to religion as well. For example, when President Bush decided to go to war with Iraq, he had the full support of many of the pastors and members of the clergy saying that this was the right thing to do. They were supporting him, praising him, and standing 100% behind him. I remember that my pastor even stood in the pulpit supporting the decision, not as openly as many of the other pastors, but it was very evident from his comments that he supported the decision as well. The President's rating in popularity skyrocketed because the mission of the war was going according to plan. He was trusting that the pastors and clergy members would stick with him through good times and bad. When the war was going well, his trust was correct; the clergy stood beside him. However, when the war turned and innocent civilians were being killed, Americans were losing their lives by the hundreds, and the expenses of the war began to impact the economy at home, President Bush quickly found that he was on an island alone. I remember watching a news special where CNN was interviewing some of the clergy members that supported President Bush prior to the start of the war. The reporters were asking the clergy members if they were still with President Bush in his decision. These clergy leaders did not recall prior public endorsements. President Bush learned the concept "Trust Everyone yet Trust No One" the hard way.

Forensic Leaders do not write blank checks of trust to banks. One of many instances in banking occurred during an incident in 1994 when I went to the bank with my sister who wanted to buy one of my co-worker's cars. This co-worker had a Honda Prelude that was given to her in 1984. The car was now approximately ten years old. She had wrecked the car several times, yet she wanted $5,000 for the car. Before we made an offer on this car, I went to the bank with my sister who was going off to college to ensure that I could get the money for the offer we were going to make. I determined that the car was worth $3,500. My sister and I went to the bank to get a loan. In order to purchase the car, I needed to co-sign the loan. The loan officer asked what type of car we were purchasing. I told him it was a Honda Prelude. He asked what the asking price was for the car. I told him we were only going to offer $3,500. He asked who owned the car. Even though I did not understand at the time why the owner of the car was important, I obliged the officer and gave him the owner's name. He said that he knew her. The loan officer proceeded to say that if owner said the car was worth $5,000, then the car was worth $5,000. The officer was willing to make us a loan in the amount sought by the seller. Had I trusted him, I would have overpaid for a car and cost my sister an additional $1,500. I got up from his office, immediately made a withdrawal, got a cashier's check for the withdrawal and opened an account at a different bank, much to the dismay of my sister.

Forensic leaders don't issue blank checks of trust in relationships. The issue of trust even occurs in relationships. Nothing distorts a leader's ability to lead more than a relationship that has gone bad. My favorite examples are families and spouses. We believe that we have to trust our family members, our spouse, and give them a blank check of trust. Being in a relationship and issuing a blank check is counter-productive to the relationship. I think that the trust we are taught to have in our personal relationships, as well as our professional relationships, does more damage than good.

It is very important that I trust my spouse and family; however, I recognize that we are all human, and anyone is subject to making a mistake. If I trust everyone but trust no one, when the trust is broken, I will not spend days, weeks or months trying to understand how and why the trust between loved ones was broken. Trust everyone one but trust no one is designed to lessen the shock in the event that betrayal does occur so that one will have the fortitude to continuing leading. Great leaders must remain strong at all times because so many people are depending on them.

Forensic leaders must apply the concept of trust everyone yet trust no one with the issue of race. It is incumbent upon the leader to understand this principle with race. Trust everyone yet trust no one when referencing race is a complicated objective to obtain. Because of slavery, the civil rights movement, the women's rights movement, and the voting rights movement, history makes it difficult for the races to trust one another. Because of prior history amongst the races, leaders continue to make horrific mistakes in their leadership style or their leadership decisions. So for this principle, I am going to take the opposite approach. When it comes to race or different cultures, we often do not trust enough.

I believe that the leaders who trust openly without trusting completely are the ones elevated to success. I remember when I bought my first car. I was so excited with the purchase. I was working the cash register at McDonald's. During this time, I had a close friend, Chuck Hutchins, who just happened to be white. His dad was president of a local bank, the People's Bank. My mom and dad did business with this bank, and my dad did not have the best credit. All of my friends at this time were buying cars. Mr. Hutchins came into the restaurant where I was working at the register to place an order. I said, "Hey, how are you doing?" He replied, "Fine. I didn't know you were working." I responded that I had been working at this restaurant for about fifteen months. He said that if he could ever do anything for me to let him know. I told him that I really needed my own transportation and that my dad and I were looking at a '78 Monte Carlo which would cost me $1,500. He said that he would take care of it for me. He said for me to tell my dad to come by the bank and sign the paperwork.

I remember going home and talking to my dad and getting the response, "That man's not going to give you a loan." Now, because of my dad's prior experiences, he had good reasons not to believe I was preapproved for a loan. I told him that Mr. Hutchens said all my dad had to do was come to the bank and sign the paperwork with me and the loan would be mine. Well, the next day we went to the bank and signed the paperwork just as Mr. Fred Hutchens had said. He handed me a check for $1,500. I purchased my first vehicle. I had to trust him. That was not the only time.

On another occasion, I was a junior in college where I had the opportunity to intern with Georgia's General Assembly. I was asked by the Dr. Well, the department chair, to apply to be an intern with the State of Georgia General Assembly. I said to myself, "I'm not going to do this. This man is just being nice to me. He is trying to reach a quota." So, I didn't fill out the application. Soon he came back to me again saying, "Trent, I didn't get your application, so I'm going to extend the deadline. I want you to fill out the application to be an intern." So I'm thinking to myself, "Why is this man harassing me just to tell me no?" Not long after, one of my favorite professors, Dr. Wagner, informed me that the committee was waiting on me to fill out my application. He said, "Trent, whenever someone asks you to do something like that, it means that it's a done deal." I didn't realize that. Dr. Wagner was also white. Of course, I filled out the application and turned it in. Of course, I received the internship which provided me one of the most enlightening educational experiences of my college career. To do so, I had to trust someone who didn't look like me, didn't act like me, or didn't even (from the outside looking in) think like me.

I remember participating in our system level leadership meeting approximately ten years ago, and we were meeting at our summer conference. At this conference, we would always discuss our school improvement plan, and the problems we needed to face as a school system. When we analyzed our test performance data, we were clear about one thing: there was a need for the system to focus on the achievement gap among the races in the schools. What we did not realize at that time was that the rest of America had the same issue. We were trying to decide how to address it and whether or not we should go public with our disparity data. I remember saying that I did not understand that if we had a school improvement plan and we had a problem as horrific as the achievement gap between our African-American and White students, why would we not put it in our school improvement plan? The superintendent, looking for guidance in the leadership staff, opened it up to the floor. What would be the pros and cons in opening this up for public discussion? I was very pleased that the superintendent allowed the discussion to move forward. Yet, on the other hand, I could not understand what the debate was. At this meeting, there were six African-American participants, and approximately fourteen white participants. To my dismay, none of the other African-Americans wanted to openly address the issue. I thought I was on an island by myself until three brave white females came to the aid of the underperforming students in our system. I am sad to say that it was not enough at that time to get it added to the plan, but thanks to President Bush and No Child Left Behind legislation, the following year we had no choice but to pay attention.

Trent,

"I am promoting Mr. North." Those words did not even register. They didn't make sense. What can be higher than a principal because he certainly can't be <u>leaving</u> our school. No, I'm not clapping. I'm not happy about this. This is <u>NOT</u> good news.

But it finally sank in. I finally comprehended. The jury is still out on whether or not it makes sense. But you are leaving us. And selfishly, I am sad.

I was so surprised and excited when I was assigned to the Middle School. I will have a fresh start. You were so enthusiastic, so supportive. You let me find my way and do my job. Thank you.

Thank you for your confidence in me as an educator. Thank you for your encouragement when I needed to grow. Thank you for creating an atmosphere where I feel at home. Yes, I do get that "welcoming ethos" thing. We thought you were crazy, but you knew all along what was needed and you succeeded.

It has been a blessing to have had these past six years with you as my principal. We've laughed and cried. Well, I cried, you consoled. And you will be greatly missed.

I wish you a great success in your new position. I know the excitement you feel because that's the way I felt coming to CMS. May your next six years be as fulfilling and rewarding as the last six have been for me.

Chevy Chase, Maryland

Chapter 9

COURAGE

Boss Man,

There is so much I could say . . . There is so much we could all say . . . But, the one thing I'll ALWAYS remember is . . . How you treat others.

Thank you for:
- A Welcoming Ethos that will NEVER die.
- Your words of wisdom, as well as your constructive criticism.
- The "memorable" field trips
  - ❖ Dessert Nights
  - ❖ Gift Baskets
  - ❖ Late Night Hotel swaps on Jekyll Island
  - ❖ You walking several blocks to purchase "Heavy Narcotics" in Savannah
- The sounds of you singing.
- Your SMILE, that will linger in the hallways of CMS and our hearts forever.
- But MOST of ALL . . . Thank you for being more than just our Boss.

  Thank you for being our FRIEND!

Gulf Shores, Alabama

Wolfram Alpha defines courage as a quality of spirit that enables you to face danger or pain without showing fear. A courageous leader can be described as fearlessness, as having fortitude, as having heart, and as having valor. All of these are terms used to describe courage. The opposite of courage is a coward, not willing to take a stand due to fear of potential consequences.

Courage is a part of almost everything we do. It shows up more than one could ever imagine. It shows up in relationships, public forums, individual conversations, group conversations, meetings and when attempting to make a decision. It is prevalent throughout the conversations or dialogue on substantive issues. Courage requires having tenacity, having the will to press forward knowing that the obstacle that lies ahead could potentially be catastrophic, potentially be career-ending, or could potentially be devastating to one's way of life. More importantly the absence of courage enables conformity to occur.

Anyone can lead. However, it is impossible to lead effectively without courage. A key characteristic of forensic leadership is courage. It is impossible to lead an organization systemically without courage. Courage is a necessary ingredient for any leadership position. Leader without courage can make small changes. However, the small changes don't last or don't lead to systemic changes. Courage is needed to allow leaders to focus on the task at hand and not allow personalities or special interests to impede the focus. Ignoring personalities and not allowing them to derail the task at hand is the most difficult principle of being a courageous leader to master.

For example, for many educators in my profession, No Child Left Behind is the worst piece of legislation to impact education and they wanted it repealed. I disagree with my profession. I believe No Child Left Behind provided public education the need to refocus priorities. We are graduating and promoting a higher quality of students.

I remember standing in front of my faculty and discussing the impact that NCLB has on public education. Discussing NCLB was not a popular topic and I had to take the focus off of President Bush who had a low approval rating at the time to focus on the law. I was able change the conversation from the man and his personality to the law itself. As the leader of the school, I was able to foster civil discourse about the benefits of NCLB, while recognizing the lack of funding to accompany the mandate.

Forensic leaders exhibit courage when dealing with politics. Some leaders are easily led by the personalities of the Democratic Party, Republican Party, spiritual leaders, Fox News, CNN News, civic leaders and other media outlets. Yes, organizations take own the identity of personalities and few leaders are able to support the other organization due to the personalities. Rosh Limbaugh is not the Republican Party and Jessie Jackson is not the Democratic Party. Every proposal by the Democratic Party is not a bad or a horrible idea, just as every proposal by the Republican Party is not a bad or horrible idea. Leaders with courage are able to see past the personality and have civil discourse about the policy and the potential good it can have for everyone while recognizing that not every policy is perfect. Forensic Leaders not only have the courage to remain focused on the issue and not the personality, but the leaders are also bold enough to support the policy publically. It takes courage to not enter into a debate as a Republican or a Democratic, and I am not referencing a political debate. Even though they are few, courageous leaders focus on policy and not personalities.

Another example is President Obama asking the CEO of General Electric, Jeff Immelt, to lead his Job Creation Task Force. GE is one of the largest employers in America, and a company that is proud about employing workers abroad. After all, the American based company is receiving about 60 percent of its profit globally. Yet, a Democratic president who is attempting to create jobs at home sought out a Republican to head this effort. The president knew that the CEO of GE was a diehard Republican, yet he called upon him for assistance. The CEO knew that the president was a Democrat and that his parents would have a problem with him assisting a Democratic president. He was quoted as saying "When I told my parents that the president had asked for my assistance, they said and you told him no—didn't you?" Without the permission from mom and dad, he agreed to head the taskforce. Strong leaders don't care who gets the credit just as long as the desired outcome is beneficial. For Jeff, the office of the White House was larger than any party.

A leader has to have courage. There are a number of leaders who are competent yet lack the skills or lack the courage to lead. Maya Angelo said it best—"Courage—without it you cannot practice the other virtues consistently."

Most people would agree that honesty is an important virtue that one should expect from its leaders; however, without consistent courage there is no true leadership. An example is the time I missed a technology meeting as the principal of the middle school. The agenda was to discuss the purchase of new technology in our system. I remember being reprimanded for not attending the meeting. Even though it was to no avail, I informed the technology director that I was not aware of the meeting. When I began to analyze the conversation, at first I was a little disappointed because I felt as if I was deliberately left out of this meeting, yet reprimanded for not being present. Even though I did not place a lot of stock in the missed meeting, I needed to understand the miscommunication to prevent it from occurring again. I began by calling a colleague, within the system. I asked him if he had attended the meeting and he replied yes. I followed by asking him how he knew about the meeting, and he stated that he received the invite in an email. I asked him to retrieve the original email. Of course he pulled it up, and my name was not on the email. I asked him if he would forward the email to me.

Even though my colleague was honest, he said no; he would not forward the email and did not. After all, who wants to correct their boss? He knew that I had received a verbal reprimand, yet he didn't want to agitate or frustrate the Director of Technology. He did not have the courage to stand up for what was correct. Please keep in mind how minor the infraction was; yet the unwillingness of a colleague to get involved and help correct a mistake. The colleague did not have the courage to do the right thing.

A new colleague of mine had just arrived in town. He and his wife were seeking a place to worship. When my friend broached the issue with me, I knew this would be a simple task. Even though Sunday mornings are the most racially divisive time in society, I consider just about all the pastors in the city and many in the county personal friends. I asked the question, "What are you looking for?" The response caught me off guard, yet impressed me. The couple was seeking a church that was diverse in its membership. Even though I am friends with many of the clergy in my community and familiar with many of our churches, I could not think of a church that could fulfill this couple's request. As the chairman of the board of directors for my church, I knew we were not a diverse congregation.

About a year later this couple finally found a church to call home, Midway Macedonia. Knowing the couple and the pastor as I do, I decided to take my family there for a special event that the church was hosting. My wife, my two daughters, and I were excited. However, upon entering the facilities and then participating in the festivities, we left saddened, feeling unwelcome and vowing to never commune with the church again. I left with a strong sense of guilt and responsibility for having placed my family in that environment.

Approximately three years later the pastor of Midway Macedonia was speaking at an event I was attending. As stated earlier, I have always considered this pastor to be a friend and leader, and just as expected, the presentation was very good. During lunch I had the opportunity to spend some quality time with the pastor, once again validating that he was a good person and great leader. We discussed his ministry and the great things that were occurring. He talked about courageous conversations the church was having in an effort to fulfill the goal of the ministry—to welcome and make the church available to everyone.

Through his leadership and with the support of church leaders and members, he began to tear down stereotypes and wrong perceptions and put strategies in place to ensure that everyone was welcome at the church. After meeting with him I was elated. Even though he never stated so to me, he knew that this was not going to be popular among some of his colleagues. He also knew that this would not be a popular change for some of his church members.

Through his leadership the church designed and displayed a billboard depicting the diversity of the church. It showed black students and white students who were members of their congregation. Some will say that color is not important, but the billboard created quiet conversations among some members of the community. It took courage for the leadership to take such a bold initiative. Prior to leaving that day, he invited me to visit his church. I never once mentioned my previous experience to him.

A year and some months later, I ran into him at a football game and he reminded me that I had not visited his church. "Mr. North, you said you were going to come and visit with us." And I recalled, "Yes, I did." I got up the two days later, put on my clothes, and went to visit his church. When I left the church I had tears in my eyes. The tears were not a reflection of a man being soft, but were the tears of, "I know it can be done in suburban communities too because I just left a church where it is occurring." When I entered the church I was greeted by people that I knew and some that I did not. I was greeted by males and females, blacks and whites. The entire ethos of the church was welcoming; I could feel it as soon as I arrived. As I parked in the parking lot and was greeted, the welcome I received this time was not the one that I had received the first time I visited. I got excited as I walked to the church. When I started to open the door the pastor's wife was there and since I was not sure if she remembered me I wanted to go in "under the radar". She did recognize me and welcomed me, but before she could do so three others from the church had welcomed me and made it a point to ensure I was able to navigate throughout the church. I was able to make my way to the 9:45 service. As I went to sit on the second row, I recognized several of my friends both black and white. In fact there was one couple that had attended my church and had since moved their membership there. It was fascinating. The service was moving. It was very evident that the Spirit was in the room. The service wasn't for show or for entertainment, but it was a perfect worshiping experience. The music was not at all what I expected it to be. It was very lively and upbeat to the point that when the pastor opened the doors of the church, I felt compelled to go and join in. I wanted to become a part of what they were doing. It wasn't about ethnicity. What they were doing was genuine. I kept telling myself, "You can't go here. You are the Chairman of the Board of Directors for your church. You can't come here. Besides, you're a deacon of your church." When I left the church I couldn't wait to get home to share with my wife the good news. Although they didn't get me to join, they do have an ambassador who visited their facilities who has nothing but great things to say about the church, the members, and everyone involved with that ministry. It took courage for the pastor to break down the walls to make certain that people who look like me feel welcome in his church. That's what courage is. It takes courage on Sunday morning, and it takes the same courage to act Monday through Friday.

In many instances identifying leaders with courage can be easy. Dr. Martin Luther King with threats made on his life continued to fight for equality. Our founding fathers, Thomas Jefferson, Benjamin Franklin, and John Adams, risked life and family to draft the Declaration of

Independence. Harriett Tubman transported slaves, risking her life and those who accompanied her on her journey. When Abraham Lincoln signed the Emancipation Proclamation, it took courage. Each is a leader with a history of courage.

Many can identify with the names listed above; however, individuals who are not well known exhibit courage every day. The female in the abusive relationship who decides to leave and seek help exhibits courage. The child who continues to go to school each day knowing the teacher and classmates will continue to verbally abuse him. The individual who chooses to seek public office knowing that failure will be public. Every day many individuals in society exhibit courage, however, it is imperative for forensic leaders to consistently exhibit courage and stand for what is right and just. Courage is the foundation of leadership.

Forensic Leaders are rare in society, yet the demands for those who are willing to go against the status quo to make a meaningful difference are great. In the new millennium, organizations today require a leadership style that reflects the complexity of today's problems and the global economy. A forensic leader can meet that task. The foundation for forensic leadership is built upon courage. Without courage, the other principles lose their effectiveness. A forensic leader has the ability to visualize the appropriate culture, convey high expectations, foster quality relationships, remain customer focused and be politically active. In order for our country, corporate America, and leaders of organizations to compete effectively, forensic leadership is demanded.

BIBLIOGRAPHY

Blanchard, Ken & Bowles, Sheldon, (2001), *High Five!,* New York, NY: HarperCollins Publishers, Inc.

Johnson, Spencer, (1998), *Who Moved My Cheese?,* New York, NY: G.P. Putnam's Sons Publishers

Maxwell, John C., (2006), *The Difference Maker,* Nashville, TN: Thomas Nelson, Inc.

Maxwell, John C., (2001), *The 17 Indisputable Laws of Teamwork,* Nashville, TN: Thomas Nelson, Inc.

Maxwell, John C., (2002), *Leadership 101,* Nashville, TN: Thomas Nelson, Inc.

Singleton, Glenn & Linton, Curtis, (2006), *Courageous Conversations,* Thousand Oaks, CA: Corwin Press

Smith, Dr, J. Alfred, Sr., (1996), *Faithful Over A Few Things,* Lithonia,GA: Orman Press

Tatum, Beverly Daniel, (1997), *Why Are All the Black Kids Sitting Together in the Cafeteria?,* New York, NY: Basic Books